ISBN 978-1-332-33043-0
PIBN 10315002

This book is a reproduction of an important historical work. Forgotten Books uses state-of-the-art technology to digitally reconstruct the work, preserving the original format whilst repairing imperfections present in the aged copy. In rare cases, an imperfection in the original, such as a blemish or missing page, may be replicated in our edition. We do, however, repair the vast majority of imperfections successfully; any imperfections that remain are intentionally left to preserve the state of such historical works.

For support please visit www.forgottenbooks.com

English
Français
Deutsche
Italiano
Español
Português

www.forgottenbooks.com

Mythology Photography **Fiction**
Fishing Christianity **Art** Cooking
Essays Buddhism Freemasonry
Medicine **Biology** Music **Ancient
Egypt** Evolution Carpentry Physics
Dance Geology **Mathematics** Fitness
Shakespeare **Folklore** Yoga Marketing
Confidence Immortality Biographies
Poetry **Psychology** Witchcraft
Electronics Chemistry History **Law**
Accounting **Philosophy** Anthropology
Alchemy Drama Quantum Mechanics
Atheism Sexual Health **Ancient History**
Entrepreneurship Languages Sport
Paleontology Needlework Islam
Metaphysics Investment Archaeology
Parenting Statistics Criminology
Motivational

ENGLISH
MEN OF SCIENCE

EDITED BY

J. REYNOLDS GREEN, Sc.D.

SIR WILLIAM FLOWER

a

W. H. Flower

BY
R. LYDEKKER

PUBLISHED IN LONDON BY
T & , AND IN NEW
YORK BY E. P. DUTTON & CO,
1906

BY

R. LYDEKKER

PUBLISHED IN LONDON BY
... AND IN NEW
YORK BY

1906

Nat. Hist

PREFACE

ALTHOUGH the complete manuscript of this volume was placed in the hands of the editor before the publication of the late Mr. C. J. Cornish's *Life of Sir William Flower* (in 1904), yet the present writer was aware that such a work was in progress, and that it would deal with the social and personal rather than with the scientific side of Sir William's career. Consequently it was decided at an early period of the work to concentrate attention in the present volume on the latter aspect of the subject; as indeed is only fitting in the case of a biography belonging to a series specially devoted to men of science. An incidental advantage of this arrangement is that the writer has been able in the main to confine himself to the discussion of topics with which he is more or less familiar, rather than to attempt to chronicle events and episodes to which he must of necessity be a stranger, and to attempt an appreciation of a fine character for which he is in no wise qualified.

It will be obvious from the above, that any references in the text to earlier biographies do not relate to Mr. Cornish's volume.

In the course of the text, it has been necessary to make certain allusions to the condition and the mode of exhibition of the specimens in the public galleries of the Zoological Department of the Natural History Museum previous to the new *régime* inaugurated by Sir William Flower. The writer may take this opportunity of stating that these are in no wise intended to convey the slightest reflection on those who had charge of the galleries previous to the new era. Technical museum-installation and display is a comparatively new thing; and the old plan of arrangement had become obsolete, not for want of attention, but because a more advanced scheme had been developed by gradual evolution, and the adoption of this involved a clean sweep.

In conclusion, the writer has to express his best thanks to Mr. C. E. Fagan, of the Secretariat of the Natural History Museum, for kindly reading and revising the proof sheets.

HARPENDEN LODGE,
      HERTS, *July* 1906.

CONTENTS

vii

Life of Flower

CHAPTER I

GENERAL SKETCH OF FLOWER'S LIFE

BORN on 30th November 1831 at his father's house, " The Hill," Stratford-on-Avon, William Henry Flower was a man who had the rare good fortune not only to make a profession of the pursuit he loved best, but likewise to attain the highest possible success in, and to be appointed to the most important and influential post connected with that profession. As he tells us in that delightful book, *Essays on Museums*, he was pleased to designate as a " museum " when a boy at home a miscellaneous collection of natural history objects, kept at first in a cardboard box, but subsequently housed in a cupboard. And as a man he became the respected head of the greatest Natural History Museum in the British Empire, if not indeed in the whole world. Very significant of his future attention to details and of the importance he attached to recording the history of every specimen received in a museum, is the fact that he compiled a carefully drawn-up catalogue of his first boyish collection.

This early and persistent taste for natural history was not, as we learn from the same collection of essays, inherited from any member of either his father's 'or his

A

mother's family, but appears to have been an "idio-pathic" development. His isolated position in this respect may, perhaps, have caused Flower in later life to notice more specially than might otherwise have been the case, how comparatively rare is the development of an ingrained taste for natural history among the adult members of the British nation. This idea was exemplified by his remarking on one occasion to the present writer that he often wondered how many persons out of every thousand he passed casually in the street, or met in social intercourse, had the slightest sympathy with, or took any real interest in the subjects which formed his own favourite pursuits and lines of thought.

As regards his parentage, his father was the late Edward Fordham Flower, who was a Justice of the Peace for his county, and from whom the son inherited his tall and stately figure and dignified bearing. Edward Flower, who was a partner in the well-known brewery at Stratford-on-Avon, was the eldest son of Richard Flower, of Marden Hill, Hertfordshire, who married Elizabeth, daughter of John Fordham, of Sandon Bury, in the same county. In 1827 Edward married Celina, daughter of John Greaves, of Radford Semele, Warwick-shire, by whom he had, with other issue, Charles Edward, late of Glencassly, Sutherlandshire, and William Henry, the subject of the present memoir.

Edward Fordham Flower was noted not only for his philanthropy, but for his efforts to abolish the bearing-rein, which in his time was neither more nor less than an instrument of downright torture to all carriage horses. As the result of his efforts in this direction, was founded in 1890, by Mr. C. H. Allen, of Hampstead, a small local society for that district and Highgate, having for its object the abolition, or at all events the mitigated use, of the bearing-rein for draught-horses of all descriptions. That body did good work in this direction for many years in the north of London; and by its means the Hampstead Vestry was induced to prohibit the use of the bearing-rein on the horses in its employ—an example subsequently followed by many large coal-owners and others connected with horses.

From this small beginning arose in 1897 the now flourishing society known as the Anti-Bearing Rein Association, of which, as was appropriate, Mr. Archibald Flower, a grandson of Edward Fordham Flower, became Co.-Hon. Secretary with Mr. Allen, while the late Duke of Westminster, and the late Sir W. H. Flower (the subject of this biography) respectively accepted the positions of Patron and President.

In all the obituary notices it is stated that William Henry was the second son of Edward Fordham and Celina Flower. This, however, as I am informed by Mr. Arthur S. Flower (the eldest son of Sir William), is not strictly the case. As an actual fact, the eldest son of the aforesaid Edward and Celina was really Richard, who died in infancy, so that Charles, who was born second, grew up as the eldest son, and William Henry as the second, whereas he was really the third.

The fair-haired and blue-eyed William not being intended to succeed his father in the business, was permitted from his early years—fortunately for zoological science—to pursue that innate love of natural history which, as we have seen, developed itself in very early years and continued unabated till the close of his career. That career naturally divides into three epochs. Firstly, the period of boyhood and early manhood; secondly, the long period of official life at the museum of the Royal College of Surgeons; and thirdly, the time during which the subject of this memoir occupied the post of Director of the Natural History Branch of the British Museum, together with the short interval which elapsed between his resignation of that position and his untimely death. To each of the latter periods a separate chapter is devoted. It has, however, been found convenient, instead of restricting the present chapter to the first epoch, to include within its limits a general sketch of Flower's whole life. A fourth chapter is assigned to the period during which he was President of the Zoological Society of London, although this was synchronous with part of the period covered by the second, and with the whole of that treated of in the third chapter. Finally, the full description of his scientific work is reserved for subsequent chapters.

According to information kindly furnished by his widow, Lady Flower, delicate health prevented William Flower from being much at school during his boyhood, and he was thus largely dependent upon his mother—a sensible and well-read woman—for his early education. He was also in the habit of accompanying his father in his rides, whereby he became much interested in all that concerns horses and their well-being. Best of all, as regards opportunity for developing a love of animal life, he was in the habit of taking long, solitary rambles in the country, thereby acquiring a knowledge of Nature which could be obtained in no other manner, and developing his powers of observation.

This innate taste for natural history appears to have been further fostered in early life by frequent intercourse with the late Rev. P. B. Brodie, an enthusiastic zoologist and geologist; but whether this took place during school or college life the writer has no means of knowing. Be this as it may, it appears that after a preliminary education, partly at home and partly at private schools, Flower matriculated at London University in 1849, (the year of his present biographer's birth), attaining honours in Zoology; and that during the same year having made up his mind to adopt the study and practice of Medicine, or of Surgery as a profession, he entered the Medical Classes at University College and became a pupil at the Middlesex Hospital. It was apparently largely, if not entirely, owing to his fondness for zoology that young Flower selected Medicine as a profession, since at the time, as indeed for many years subsequently, this was practically the only career open to young naturalists devoid of sufficient private means whereby they might hope to be able to devote a certain amount of time and attention to the pursuits—and more especially Comparative Anatomy—towards which their inclinations tended.

At University College Flower had a distinguished career, gaining the gold medal in Dr. Sharpey's class of Physiology and Anatomy, and the silver medal in Zoology and Comparative Anatomy; the gold medal in the latter subjects having been carried off the same year by his fellow-student, Joseph Lister, who in after years became the distinguished surgeon, and, as Lord Lister, was for some time President of the Royal Society of London. In 1851—the year of the Great Exhibition—Flower passed his first M.B. examination at London University, coming out in the first division. In the same year he made a tour in Holland and Germany, while in 1853 he visited France and the north of Spain ; bringing home in both instances numerous sketches in pencil and sepia of the scenery and people of the countries traversed.

In all the obituary notices of Flower that have come under the present writer's notice, it is stated that he obtained the post of Curator of the museum of the Middlesex Hospital after his return from the Crimea. This is, however, proved to be incorrect by his first zoological paper, " On the Dissection of a Species of Galago," which was contributed to the Zoological Society of London in 1852, and appeared in the *Proceedings* of that body for the same year, where the author describes himself as the holder of the post in question. As a matter of fact, he was elected Curator in 1854, and resigned the post in 1854.[1]

Flower never took the degree of M.D., but three years after passing his M.B. he became (on 27th March 1854) a member of the Royal College of Surgeons of England.

A few weeks after this event a call was made for additional surgeons for the army then serving in the Crimea, and young Flower, partly, perhaps, from patriotic motives, and partly with a view of extending his practical experience in surgery, promptly volunteered his services, which were accepted. After spending a few

---

[1] The writer is indebted to the Secretary of the Middlesex Hospital for these particulars.

idle months with the Depôt Battalion then stationed at Templemore, in Ireland, he was gazetted as Assistant-Surgeon to the 63rd (now the First Battalion of the Manchester) Regiment; and in July 1854 embarked with his regiment at Cork for Constantinople. On its arrival in the east the regiment was at once hurried up to join the main army at Varna, whence it proceeded to take part in the expedition to the Crimea, where both officers and men suffered severely from exposure to the inclemencies of the climate and an insufficient commissariat during the early months of the campaign. For ten weeks together, it is reported, neither officers or men took off their clothes, either by night or by day, and for the first three weeks all ranks were compelled to get such sleep as they could obtain on the bare ground. Flower, who was present at the battles of the Alma, of Inkerman, and of Balaclava, as well as at the fall of Sebastopol, underwent many and thrilling experiences during the campaign, alike in the field and in the hospital. The hardships and privations which caused the strength of his regiment to be reduced by nearly one-half within the short period of four months, could not but tell severely on the constitution of the young surgeon, which was never very robust; and from some of the effects of these he suffered throughout his life. Nevertheless, in spite of all this, in the intervals of duty, Flower, with but scant materials at his disposal, managed to find time and energy sufficient to make a considerable number of vivid pen-and-ink, or dashes of ink-and-water, sketches of his surroundings, including one of his own tent overturned by the terrible snow-storm of 14th November 1854, and a second of the wrecked condition of the camp in general at the end of the tempest. A panoramic view of Constantinople and a sketch of the military hospital at Scutari were also among his artistic productions at this period. In recognition of his services, Flower, after being invalided home, received from the hands of Her Majesty, Queen Victoria, the Crimean medal, with clasps for the Alma, Inkerman, Balaclava, and Sebastopol; while he was also permitted to accept from H.M., the Sultan, the Turkish war-medal.

Apparently Flower had never entertained the idea of taking up the profession of an army surgeon as a permanency, and after his return to London he definitely resigned military service, with the intention of settling down to private medical practice in the Metropolis. In the spring of 1857 he passed the examination qualifying for the Fellowship of the Royal College of Surgeons; and about this time, or perhaps immediately on his return to London, he joined the staff of the Middlesex Hospital as Demonstrator in Anatomy. During the next year (1858) he was elected to the post of Assistant-Surgeon to the same Institution, where he resumed the Curatorship of the museum and was also appointed Lecturer on Comparative Anatomy. Although a large portion of his time while at the hospital was devoted to surgical and other duties connected with the medical profession, his Lectureship and Curatorship required that he should devote a considerable amount of attention to the more congenial study of Comparative Anatomy.

It was during his connection with the Middlesex Hospital that his first scientific work was published, this being the well-known and useful little volume entitled *Diagrams of the Nerves of the Human Body*, which appeared in 1861, and has passed through three editions. During this period of his career he also contributed to Holmes' *System of Surgery* an article on " Injuries to the Upper Extremities," which contained certain original observations· with regard to dislocations of the shoulder-joint ; and he likewise wrote an essay on the same subject to the Pathological Society, as well as several articles on various surgical subjects to the medical journals of the day. But even at this comparatively early period of his career Flower's published scientific work was by no means strictly confined to his ostensible profession, for his two first papers on Comparative Anatomy—the one " On the Dissection of a Galago" (Lemur) ; and the other " On the Posterior Lobes of the Cerebrum of the Quadrumana "—appeared during the period in question. During this period, as the writer of his obituary notice in the " Record " of the Royal Society well remarks, there is little doubt that Flower had breathing time, after his Crimean experiences, to collect his energies and gather up a store of valuable information which stood him in good stead in later years, when he had frequently less leisure to devote to pure study.

It was, moreover, during his official connection with the Middlesex Hospital that Mr. Flower married Georgina Rosetta, the youngest daughter of the late Admiral W. H. Smyth, C.S.I., etc., a well-known astronomer, who was for some time Hydrographer to the Admiralty and likewise Foreign Secretary to the Royal Society, the wedding taking place in 1858 at the church of Stone, in Buckinghamshire, near the bride's home. This happy union had in many ways an important influence upon the future career of the young surgeon, for, in addition to her father, several of the relatives of Mrs. (now Lady) Flower were more or less intimately connected with scientific work and scientific people ; among them being Sir Warrington Smyth (sometime Inspector-General of Mines), Professor Piazzi Smyth, General Sir Henry Smyth, and Sir George Baden Powell. It was to Lady Flower that Sir William dedicated his last work, the volume entitled *Essays on Museums*. A tour through Belgium and up the Rhine followed the marriage.

Although it scarcely comes within the purview of this biography to allude to the issue of this marriage, it may be mentioned that of the three sons born to Sir William Flower, the second alone, Stanley Smyth, inherited his father's zoological tastes. Captain S. S. Flower (who takes his first name from Dean Stanley, of Westminster, an intimate friend of the family, after serving for some time in the 5th Fusileers, obtained the appointment of Director of the Royal Museum at Bangkok, Siam, after which he was made Director of the Khedival Zoological Gardens at Giza, near Cairo, to which post (which he still holds) was subsequently added that of Superintendent of Game Protection in the Sudan. Captain Flower has not only raised the menagerie at Giza to a high state of perfection, but has contributed several papers to the *Proceedings* of the Zoological Society of London on the zoology of Siam and the Malay countries.

To revert to the proper subject of this memoir, during his tenure of the aforesaid official posts at the Middlesex Hospital it was apparent to his intimate scientific friends—among whom were included the late Professor T. H. Huxley and the late Mr. George Busk—that the inclinations of Flower were all on the side of comparative anatomy rather than towards practical surgery or medicine. Accordingly, when the appointment of Conservator to the Museum of the Royal College of Surgeons became vacant in 1861 by the death of Mr. Quekett, Flower was strongly recommended by Huxley (then Hunterian Professor), Busk, and other friends as a suitable successor, and was in due course elected by the Council. When, nine years later (1870), Huxley himself felt compelled by the pressure of other engagements and work to resign the Hunterian Professorship, the Conservator of the Museum was appointed to the vacant chair, thus once more bringing together two posts which had been sundered since Owen's resignation.

On his appointment to the Conservatorship of the Museum of the College of Surgeons, Flower once for all definitely abandoned medicine as a profession, and determined to devote the whole of his energies for the future to the study of his beloved comparative anatomy and zoology. Nevertheless, he always remained in touch with his old profession, as he was always in sympathy with those who were actively practising the same. Indeed, since the collections under his charge included a large pathological series, while during his tenure of office a large display of surgical instruments was added to the exhibits, he could not, even had he so desired, cut himself entirely adrift from old associations and old studies.

Since a considerable amount of space in a later chapter is devoted to Flower's work as Museum Curator and as Hunterian Lecturer, it will be unnecessary to allude further to it in this place, although it will be appropriate to quote the elogium on his efforts in this sphere, pronounced by the President of the Royal Society, when bestowing the Royal Gold Medal in recognition of his services to zoology.

"It is very largely due," runs the address, "to his incessant and well-directed labour that the museum of the Royal College of Surgeons at present contains the most complete, the best ordered, and the most accessible collection of materials for the study of vertebrate structures extant."

As regards his Hunterian lectures, it has been well remarked that few could have any idea of the amount of labour they involved, nor would any one be likely to guess this from the ever-ready and earnest efforts of the lecturer to give to others that knowledge he had so laboriously, and yet so pleasantly, acquired within the walls of the museum.

In addition to the official Hunterian lectures, Flower during this portion of his career commenced the delivery, as opportunity occurred, of lectures of a much more popular description, at the Royal Institution and elsewhere, by means of which he appealed to a wider audience than any that could be attracted to technical discourses, and at the same time was enabled to give a wide circulation to the discussion of subjects connected with his own special studies which had more or less of a general interest. In one of his earlier discourses of this type he discussed at considerable detail the deformities produced in the human foot by badly-designed boots or other covering among both civilised and barbarous nations. Indeed, "fashion in deformity" was at all times a favourite theme with the Hunterian Professor; and in a lecture on this subject he uttered, for him, a strong protest against the evils caused by the corset among European females, illustrating his remarks with a ghastly figure of a female skeleton distorted by the undue pressure of that fashionable article of costume.

In 1871, and again in later years, Professor Flower acted as Examiner in Zoology for the Natural Science Tripos at Cambridge, where his suave and dignified manner, and innate courtliness rendered him as great a favourite as in the Metropolis. He was during some portion of his career Examiner in Anatomy at the Royal College of Veterinary Surgeons.

Flower's official connection with the museum of the Royal College of Surgeons was brought to a close by Owen's resignation of the Post of Superintendent of the Natural History Department of the British Museum, when it was felt by all that the efficient and successful administrator of the smaller museum in Lincoln's Inn Fields, was the one man specially fitted in every way to have supreme charge of the larger establishment in the Cromwell Road. Professor Flower was accordingly selected by the three principal trustees—the Archbishop of Canterbury, the Lord Chancellor, and the Speaker of the House of Commons—to fill this important post, into the duties of which he entered during the same year. His administration of the museum—which lasted until he was compelled by failing health to send in his resignation a few months before his death—is fully discussed in the fourth chapter, and was in every way a complete success.

During his long and successful official career Sir William was the recipient of a number of honours (in addition to the medals he received for his Crimean service), and he was likewise on the roll of the more important societies connected with the branches of biological study in which he was specially interested.

Of the Royal Society Sir William was elected a Fellow in 1864—at the relatively early age of thirty-three—and he served on the Council of that body for three separate periods, namely from 1868 to 1870, from 1876 to 1878, and again from 1884 to 1886, while in 1884 and 1885 he was one of the Vice-Presidents. In 1882 his conspicuous services to zoological science was recognised by the bestowal upon him of a Royal Gold Medal—one of the most honourable distinctions in the gift of the Society; the other recipient in the same year of a similar honour being Lord Rayleigh. In handing to Professor Flower this medal, the President dwelt upon the value of his contributions to both zoology and anthropology, referring, in connection with the former science, to his paper on the classification of the Carnivora, and, in respect to the latter, to the then recently published first part of the "Catalogue of Osteological Specimens in the Museum of the Royal College of Surgeons," in which descriptions and measurements of between 1300 and 1400 human skulls are recorded. The present writer has been informed that Flower refused to be nominated for the Presidentship of the Royal Society, owing to the fear that the calls made upon his time by that office would interfere with his official duties. Of the Zoological Society Professor Flower became a Fellow so long ago as the year 1851, that is to say, three years previous to the commencement of his Crimean service. After serving for several periods on the Council he was elected to the honourable (and honorary) office of President on the death of the Marquis of Tweeddale in 1879, and in this important position he remained till his death. It should be added that Flower never received one of the medals of the Zoological Society, and this for the very good reason that such rewards are bestowed in recognition of gifts to the Society's Menagerie, and not for contributions to zoological knowledge. Flower's contributions to both the *Transactions* and the *Proceedings* of the Society were numerous, and, needless to say, valuable ; the earliest in the former having been published in 1866, and in the latter in 1852. With very few exceptions, these communications relate to mammals. Fuller details with regard to Sir William's Presidency of the Zoological Society will be found in a later chapter.

Of the Linnean Society, Flower was elected a Fellow in 1862, but he does not appear to have ever taken any active part in the administration of that body, or to have contributed to its publications, although for a time he was a Vice-President.

Tò the Geological Society, on the other hand, of which he became a Fellow in the year 1886, Sir William contributed three papers on paleontological subjects, by far the most important of which was one on the affinities and probable habits of the extinct Australian marsupial *Thylacoleo*. Further allusion to this is made in the sequel. Of the other two, one recorded the occurrence of teeth of the bear-like *Hyænarctus* in the Red Crag of Suffolk, and the other that of a skull of the manatee-like *Halitherium* in the same formation.

Of the Anthropological Institute of Great Britain and Ireland Flower was elected a Vice-President in 1879, while in 1883 he succeeded to the Presidential chair, and occupied that position till 1885. Of his numerous contributions to anthropological science, many appeared in the journal of the Institute.

In the annual meetings of the British Association for the advancement of science, Flower, from an early date, took a lively interest. At the Norwich meeting, in 1868, he acted as Vice-President of the section of Biology, while he was President of the same section at the Dublin meeting of 1878. At York he presided over the section of Anthropology in 1881; he was a Vice-President at the Aberdeen meeting of 1885, while for the second time he occupied the Presidential chair of the Anthropological section in 1894 at Oxford, when his opening address on Anthropological progress displayed great breadth of thought and generalisation. Finally, he was President of the Association at the meeting held in Newcastle-on-Tyne in 1889, his address at the latter meeting forming the first article in *Essays on Museums*.

Among other offices of a kindred nature to the above, it may be mentioned that Sir William was President of the section of Anatomy at the International Medical Congress held in London in August 1881. His address on that occasion (reprinted as article 7 of the volume just cited) being on the Museum of the Royal College of Surgeons. In July 1893 he acted as President of the Museum's Association at their London meeting, when, after referring to the general scope of that body, and a brief survey of some of the chief museums of Europe, he sketched out a plan for an ideal building of this nature. This address also appears in *Essays on Museums*. Sir William, the year before his death, had also undertaken to preside over the meeting of the International Zoological Congress held at Cambridge in the summer of 1898, but was prevented by failing health ; his place being filled by Lord Avebury (Sir John Lubbock). On 29th November 1895, Sir William Flower delivered an address at the opening of the Perth Museum, in which he pointed out the special function of local museums. Five years earlier (3rd November 1890) he had delivered another address on a very similar occasion, namely, the opening of the Booth Museum, in the Dyke Road, Brighton, famed for its unrivalled collection of British birds, the great majority of which had been shot and subsequently mounted in a most artistic manner by its founder. This splendid collection, it may be mentioned, was bequeathed at Mr. Booth's death to the British Museum, but it was reluctantly declined by the Trustees, who waived their right in favour of the Corporation of Brighton. At the end of October 1896, Sir William, then in failing health, somewhat rashly undertook a journey to Scotland to assist Lord Reay in the inauguration of the Gatty Marine Laboratory at St. Andrews.

Another important address delivered by Flower was one read before the Church Congress at their meeting, held in October 1883, at Reading, on " Recent Advances in Natural Science in Relation to the Christian Faith." It is reprinted in *Essays on Museums*. In this address Flower, while proclaiming his full adherence to the doctrine of the transmutation of species and the evolution of every organic form from a pre-existing type, urged that this did not in the least shake his confidence in all the essential teaching of the Christian religion. At the

B

same time he pointed out that the new doctrine in no wise detracted from the position of the Divine Ruler of the world as the controller, and indeed the originator, of animal development.

Shortly after his retirement from the post of Conservator, Professor Flower was elected a Trustee of the Hunterian Collection of the Royal College of Surgeons. Many years later, in 1881, he became a Trustee of Sir John Soane's Museum, in Lincoln's Inn Fields.

Mention has already been made of the fact that in an early stage of his career Sir William became an M.B. of London, and that later on he was elected to the Fellowship of the Royal College of Surgeons. In addition to these professional qualifications, he was also the recipient of honorary degrees from the two elder Universities. Thus in 1891 he was made a D.C.L. of Oxford, the public orator of the University, when the degree was conferred, acclaiming him as a living proof of the truth of the old saying, ἀρχή ἄνδρα δείξει, attributed to one of the seven wise men of Greece, and as a man who had passed with increasing distinction from one important official post to another ; and he was likewise a D.Sc. of Cambridge. But this by no means exhausts the list of his academic honours, Edinburgh, St. Andrews, and Trinity College, Dublin, claiming him on their roll of honorary LL.D.'s, while in 1889 he received from Durham the degree of D.C.L. The Edinburgh degree, it may be mentioned, was conferred on the occasion of the celebration of the tercentenary of the University. Sir William was also a Ph.D.

Nor were Flower's conspicuous services to zoological science suffered to remain unrecognised by the Government of his country, for he was created a C.B. in 1887, three years after his first appointment to the British Museum, and five years later (1892) followed the higher distinction of the K.C.B. But this does not exhaust the list of official honours, for in 1887 Sir William received from Her Majesty, the late Queen Victoria, the Jubilee Medal. Had he lived to the date of its foundation, it is possible that Flower might have been admitted by his Sovereign as one of the original members of the Order of Merit.

From His Majesty the German Emperor Sir William Flower received the distinction of the Royal Prussian order, "Pour la Mérite," an honour of which he was justly very proud. As a distinguished friend pointed out in his letter of congratulation on learning of the new distinction, "it is the one European decoration which an Englishman may be proud to wear, and bestowed, as I believe it to be, with the sanction of the very few who have already got it. It is the one order which real work, apart from rank and wealth and courtiers' trick, alone can win." As another eminent friend described it on the same occasion, it is truly "the blue riband of literary and scientific decorations."

Numerous foreign scientific societies, it is almost unnecessary to observe, were proud to claim the name of Sir William Flower on the list of their honorary members or associates. It is however by no means easy to give a complete list of these honourable distinctions, for Flower was not one who followed the fashion of adding every possible combination of letters to his name in every book or paper he wrote. Perhaps the most important of these distinctions was that of Foreign Correspondent of the Institute of France. Among other societies and academies to which he belonged, were those of the Netherlands, Sweden, and Belgium.

Although Flower's scientific writings are discussed at length in the later chapters of this memoir, it may be mentioned in this place that during the " eighties " he contributed an important series of articles to the ninth edition of the "Encyclopædia Britannica." At the commencement of that great undertaking, although the article " Ape " was confided to the competent hands of the late Professor St. George Mivart, some of the other articles, such as the one on " Antelope," were entrusted to writers who, whatever their other merits may have been, had certainly no claim to be regarded as specialists on the subject of mammals. It was not long before this was recognised by the publishers, who forthwith engaged for this section of the work the services of Flower, supplemented by those of the late Dr. Dobson and Mr. O. Thomas. Among the more important articles by Flower were those on the Horse, Kangaroo, Lemur, Lion, Mammalia (in co-operation with Dr. Dobson), Megatherium, Otter, Platypus, Rhinoceros, Seal, Tapir, and Whale. These and other articles, together with the one on Ape by Professor Mivart and several on the smaller mammals by Mr. Thomas, were subsequently combined and revised to form the basis of the *Study of Mammals Living and Extinct*, by Sir William Flower and the present writer, and was published by Messrs. A. & C. Black in 1891, which long formed the standard English work on the subject, although now, owing to the rapid progress in zoology and the great change which has taken place in nomenclature, is somewhat out of date.

The excellent little volume on *The Horse* in Sir John Lubbock's (Lord Avebury) *Modern Science Series*, published in 1891, and the *Essays on Museums* (1898), also appeared during this portion of Flower's career.

Although so largely occupied in the study of mammals and other creatures from distant parts of the world, Sir William never travelled much, and never visited little known regions or did any important collecting abroad. In addition to his Crimean experiences, and the journeys in Holland, France, and the Rhine country, to which allusion has been already made, his foreign tours appear to have been but few. In the winter of 1873-74 he was, however, enabled to enjoy a trip up the Nile in company with Mrs. Flower, and he visited Biarritz in 1892. During the former excursion he made a number of sketches which bear ample testimony to his powers as an artist. With his great knowledge of anatomy, it may be here mentioned, coupled with his skill with the pencil, he enjoyed a great advantage over many contemporary zoologists in being able to draw accurate and life-like portraits of the animals he loved so well. Nevertheless, if only from lack of time, he never attempted to illustrate with his own hand any of his numerous scientific contributions —at all events in later years. Owing to need for complete rest, after a short sojourn in the early part of 1897 at Marazion, on the south coast of Cornwall, he spent much of the following winter abroad; and after his resignation of the Directorship of the Museum in 1898, he spent the following winter at San Remo, from which he returned less than two months before his death.

As regards the closing scenes of his life, a very few words must suffice. For the last two years of his existence he had evidently been in failing health, largely due to his incessant exertions and from his refusal to spare himself, even when warned of the absolute necessity of so doing by his medical adviser. In August 1898, after a long period during which he had been compelled to devote little or no attention to his official duties, he placed his resignation of the Directorship of the Museum in the hands of the Trustees. The aforesaid sojourn at San Remo during the following winter effected some slight temporary improvement in his health, but on his return to London, in May 1899, it was painfully apparent that his constitution—never too robust—was shattered beyond hope of permanent recovery. And, after a slight temporary rally, from his malady of heart-failure, a sharp relapse occurred on Thursday, 29th June, followed by pneumonia, and on Saturday, 1st July, Sir William Flower passed peacefully away, at the age of sixty-seven years, at his residence, 26 Stanhope Gardens, London.

A memorial service was held on the following Wednesday at St. Luke's Church, Sidney Street, Chelsea, which was attended by a large and sympathetic congregation of friends and scientific men, including Sir Edward Maunde Thompson, the Chief Librarian and Director of the British Museum, and Professor E. Ray Lankester, Sir William's successor in the Directorship of the Natural History Branch of the same.

Sir William was undoubtedly a man of high and noble character, endeared to all with whom he was brought into intimate relations by his unfailing courtesy and charm of manner. To the present writer, it may be said perhaps without undue egotism, he was a friend and counsellor such as cannot be expected more than once in a life-time.

No better summary of Sir William's general character and high attributes can perhaps be given (certainly the present writer cannot attempt to rival it) than the one drawn up by his biographer in the " Year-book " of the Royal Society for 1901, which may accordingly be quoted *in extenso* :—

" In private life no one was more beloved and esteemed. He was in every sense a domestic man, finding the highest joys that life brought him with his family and children. The same courtly bearing and high tone, the same preference for all that was good, was in private circles mingled with the same genial smile, the fascinating account of something interesting or novel, and the respect and deference to others, which was part of his upright, unselfish nature. Many a young naturalist will gratefully remember the kind encouragement and valued advice he was ever ready to offer, and the stimulus which the sympathetic interest of a leader in the department gave him.

" In the busy life of Sir William and in the constant calls on brain and nervous system—strong though these were—there came times when a feeling of lassitude with headache and spinal uneasiness, if not prostration, showed that the indoor life and the strain of many duties had told with severity both on the central nervous system and on the heart. His annual holiday sufficed in many cases to recruit his energies, especially when he visited Scotland and the charming home of his friends,

Mr. and Mrs. Drummond, of Megginch. There he met other friends, such as Dean and Lady Augusta Stanley [after whom a son and a daughter were respectively named] and Colonel Drummond-Hay, of Seggieden, brother of Mr. Drummond. Moreover, he was always interested in the splendid collection of birds made by Colonel Drummond-Hay during his wanderings with the Black Watch."

Another passage from the same memoir of his life runs as follows :—

" One side of Sir William's life deserves special notice, viz., his social influence, and the endeavour to popularise the great institution with which he was officially connected. These influences, developed at the Museum of the College of Surgeons with great success, were brought to bear on a much wider circle in connection with the National Museum and as President of the Zoological Society ; and no one was more fitted than he —either for the courtly circle or the large gatherings of working men who flocked on Saturday afternoons to the galleries of the museum. In all his many and varied social functions in his prominent positions he was ably seconded by one who identified herself with his every engagement, and to whom his last volume of collected addresses was dedicated. A man of wide sympathies, he is found at one time addressing a Civil Service dinner, at another a Volunteer gathering, now descanting on evolution to a Church Congress, and again speaking at a Mayoral banquet, a girls' school, or an industrial exhibition. The strain on his physique demanded by these efforts would have been great to an ordinary man, but it must have been serious to one whose main energies were heavily taxed by exhausting scientific work. His powerful constitution was thus slowly but surely sapped, yet to an eager mind and a generous heart, such as his, little heed was paid to himself.

. . . . . .

" Taken all in all, we shall not soon see so talented and so accurate a comparative anatomist, so impressive a speaker, so facile an artist, or a public man with a higher type of character."

The zoological and anthropological side of Sir William's work (with which the present writer is more competent to deal than he is with his social relations and character) is discussed at length in later chapters of this memoir; but a few observations may be here introduced on subjects which scarcely come within the category of purely scientific work.

At intervals during his life-time Flower communicated a considerable number of letters to the *Times* and other journals on topics more or less intimately connected with animals and animal life. His sympathy with the crusade against the tight bearing-rein, initiated by his father, has already received mention. Equally marked was his sympathy with the movement against the wearing by ladies of the plumage of birds (other than game-birds, etc.), and more especially the so-called " osprey plumes " —really the breeding-plumes of the egrets and white herons—in the so-called decoration of their bonnets and hats. The extreme cruelty involved—at least in the case of the " ospreys "—in this practice, which entails the destruction of the birds during the nesting-season, when these nuptial plumes are alone donned, and consequently in many instances the destruction of the helpless young by slow starvation, was painted in forcible language by more than one letter from Flower's pen. Happily, as the result of these and other letters from sympathetic naturalists, and the foundation of the Society for the Protection of Birds (whose general aims were likewise strongly advocated by Sir William), this detestable practice has been much diminished of late years, although very much remains to be done in this way before there can be any pretence of saying that birds, even in this country, are treated by man as they deserve.

On another occasion he wrote, deprecating the wholesale destruction of bottle-nosed whales, which had been advocated on account of the enormous quantities of fishes devoured by these cetaceans. The question of pelagic sealing in Bering Sea, and the best way of preventing unnecessary slaughter, and thus eventual extermination, of the sea-bears and sea-lions which visit the Pribiloff Islands, also occupied his attention. And to him was confided the duty of selecting the naturalists (Professor d'Arcy Thompson and Captain Barrett-Hamilton) who represented British interests in the International Commission despatched to those islands in 1896 and 1897, to report on the sealing generally and the habits of the sea-bears, or fur-seals.

The best mode of disposing of the bodies of the dead was also a subject to which Sir William devoted a share of his attention, and he was a strong advocate for cremation, or, failing this, for burial in wicker caskets in light sandy soil.

The effects of the weather on " Cleopatra's Needle " a comparatively short time after it had been set up on the Thames Embankment; the best means of utilising and beautifying the gardens in Lincoln's Inn Fields; and the anomaly that while a heavy book could be sent by post for a few pence, the charge on a heavy letter, at the time in question, was considerable, were among many other miscellaneous topics upon which he wrote.

In conversation it was Sir William's great delight, whenever possible, to turn the subject to his own particular studies and pursuits; but, as mentioned by an exalted personage on an occasion referred to in the sequel, he never wearied his hearers. In a new or rare animal, his delight was almost childish; and the present writer has often reflected how intense would have been his pleasure had he been spared to see the first specimen brought to this country of that wonderful animal, the okapi of the Semliki Forest.

To his official subordinates Sir William was also readily accessible—possibly almost too much so; and he had always a word of praise for work faithfully carried out under his direction, even if, from a slight misunderstanding of his instructions, it had not been executed precisely on the lines he himself would have desired. He was never above lending a hand himself at manual work; and the writer well recollects an occasion at the museum where a large animal was, with some difficulty, being moved, and Sir William, although at the time manifestly unfit for severe physical effort, would insist upon aiding in the task.

As a host, Sir William Flower, ably seconded by Lady Flower, had few rivals and no superiors; and although he absolutely detested tobacco, such was his good-nature, that he would not deny his male friends the luxury of an after-dinner cigarette—the idea of ladies smoking would probably have been too much even for his good-nature and tolerance of other people's little weaknesses.

This chapter may be fitly brought to a close by referring to the fact that it was largely owing to the advocacy of Sir William that a statue of his intimate friend Huxley was placed in the Central Hall of the Natural History Museum, in company with those of Darwin and Owen, so that "Huxley and Owen, often divided in their lives, would come together after death in the most appropriate place and amidst the most appropriate surroundings." In this Valhalla of men pre-eminent in British biological science of the nineteenth century, Flower's own bust has found its home; but of this more anon.

In this connection it may be added that Sir William Flower wrote for the *Proceedings* of the Royal Society the obituary notice of Sir Richard Owen, who had been his predecessor in his own two most important offices. Despite the fact that Flower had been instrumental in overthrowing at least one of Owen's " pet theories," this biographical notice is written in the kindest and most sympathetic spirit, giving full credit to the "immense labours and brilliant talents" of this truly remarkable man.

An earlier obituary notice from Flower's pen which appeared in the same journal was devoted to a sketch of the life of George Rolleston, the brilliant Professor of Anatomy and Physiology of Oxford, whose comparatively early death in 1881 was one of the real losses to biological science.

Of a more varied and popular nature were Flower's

reminiscences of his friend Huxley, which appeared in the *North American Review* for September 1895. A fourth biographical notice was the "eulogium" on Charles Darwin, delivered by Sir William at the centenary meeting of the Linnean Society, held on 24th May 1888, in which the speaker acknowledged the incomparable importance of Darwin's work, and incidentally avowed his own acceptance of the doctrine of evolution. Compared to Darwin's achievements, he observed, "most of the work which we others do is but irregular, guerilla warfare, attacks on isolated points, mere outpost skirmishing, while his was the indefatigable, patient, unintermittent toil, conducted in such a manner and on such a scale that it could scarcely fail to secure victory in the end."

CHAPTER II

[1861-1884.]

THE death, in 1861, of the eminent histological anatomist, Professor Quekett, rendered vacant the important post of Conservator of the Museum of the Royal College of Surgeons of England in Lincoln's Inn Fields. This museum, it is almost superfluous to mention, was founded by the great anatomist, John Hunter, and is hence often known popularly, although not officially, as the Hunterian Museum.

" Originally a private collection," observed Flower in his Presidential address to the Anatomical section of the International Medical Congress, held in London in the summer of 1881, " embracing a large variety of objects, it has been carried out and increased upon much the same plan as that designed by the founder, with modifications only to suit some of the requirements of advancing knowledge. The only portion of Hunter's biological collection which have been actually parted with are the stuffed birds and beasts, which, with the sanction of the Trustees appointed by the Government to see that the college performs its part of the contract as custodians of the collection, were transferred to the British Museum, and a considerable number of dried vascular preparations, which having become useless in consequence of the deterioration in their condition, resulting from age and

31

decay, have been replaced by others preserved by better methods."

In regard to the special purposes served by this museum, it is mentioned in the same address that it is maintained by the College of Surgeons "for the benefit not only of its own members, but for that of the profession at large, and indeed of all who take any interest in biological science, whether the young student preparing for his examination, or the advanced worker who has here found materials for many an important contribution by which the boundaries of knowledge have been materially enlarged. To all such it is freely open without fee or charge. Even the written or personal introduction of members, still nominally required, is never asked for on the four open days from any intelligent or interested visitor; and on the one day of the week on which it is closed for cleaning, facilities are always given to those who are desirous of making special studies, and to the increasing number of lady students, whether artistic, scholastic, or medical. Artists continually resort to the museum to find opportunities of studying anatomy of man and animals, which no other place in London affords; and of late years it has been the means of a still wider diffusion of knowledge, by the visits which have been organised on summer Saturday afternoons by various associations of artizans, to whom a popular demonstration of its contents is usually given by the Conservator."

Elsewhere in the same address we find the following passage in connection with the teaching functions of this body :—

"The various professorships and lectureships that

are attached to the College have grown up chiefly in consequence of one of the conditions under which the Hunterian Collection was entrusted to it by Government —that a course of no less than twenty-four lectures shall be delivered annually by some member of the College upon Comparative Anatomy and other subjects, illustrated by the preparations."

For some years previously to Professor Quekett's death the offices of Conservator of the Museum of the College and of Hunterian Professor of Anatomy had been disassociated ; the occupant of the professorial chair at the date in question being the late Professor T. H. Huxley, while, as already mentioned, Quekett held the Conservatorship.   At an earlier date the two offices had, however, been held conjointly ; Owen having fulfilled the duties of both for a period of no less than twenty-five years.

It may be added that, from the varied nature of the collections under his charge, the Conservator is expected to have a knowledge not only of comparative anatomy and zoology, but likewise of palæontology, physiology, surgery, and pathology.

Such a wide range of knowledge is possible to few men at the present day, but it was possessed to a very considerable extent by Mr. Flower, even at this comparatively early stage of his career ; and as the appointment was congenial to his tastes, he applied for, and in due course was elected to, the Conservatorship.   The acceptance of this involved the complete abandonment of practice as a surgeon—a course of action which, I believe, was never regretted.   For eight years Mr. Flower discharged the duties of the Conservatorship to

c

the satisfaction of the Council of the College; and when, in 1869, Professor Huxley found himself compelled by the pressure of other duties to relinquish the Hunterian chair, Flower was elected in 1870 to fill the vacancy. He thus, for the first time in his career, became entitled to the designation of "Professor," and he continued to hold the two offices till his transference to the British Museum. Here it may perhaps be well to mention, in order to avoid confusion, that in the early part of Flower's official career at the College of Surgeons the post of Articulator to the museum was held by a namesake—Mr. James Flower.

For the first eight years of his connection with the museum in Lincoln's Inn Fields the time and attention of Flower were almost entirely devoted to the improvement, augmentation, and rearrangement of the collections under his charge; and even when his duties as Hunterian Professor claimed a large share of his time, no efforts were spared to maintain the former rate of progress in the museum.

To record in detail the improvements and alterations made in the museum under Flower's able administration would obviously not only occupy a large amount of space but would, likewise, be wearisome to the reader. Attention will therefore be concentrated on a few salient features in connection with his work.

Although the anatomy of man naturally took a prominent place in what used to be called the "physiological" series, yet the preparations illustrating this subject were in the main restricted to the viscera; the details of regional anatomy and of the arrangement and distribution of muscles, vessels, and nerves not finding a place in the original scheme of the museum. This appeared to Flower to be a serious omission, and he soon set to work to exhibit human anatomy—largely on account of its paramount importance to the members of the medical profession—on a much more extensive scale than was previously the case, thereby affording by means of permanent preparations a ready demonstration, accessible at all times, of the structure of every part of the human frame. To those who have already learnt their anatomy, it has been well remarked, and who wish to refresh their memory, or verify a fact about which some passing doubt may be felt, or to those who are precluded by circumstances from visiting the dissecting room, the preparations of this series must prove of great value.

In connection with this series may be mentioned the fact that Flower published during the year he took office the work which heads the list of his numerous scientific contributions, namely, *Diagrams of the Nerves of the Human Body, exhibiting their Origin, Divisions and Connections*, which was favourably received by the medical profession. In the preparation of the anatomical series, Flower's almost unrivalled powers of dissection stood him in good stead, and it was probably during this period of his career that he first acquired the rudiments of that originality and care in museum arrangement and display that led to his being called in after life by a German savant " the Prince of Museum Directors."

Perhaps, however, the portion of the museum under his charge in which Flower was most deeply interested was that devoted to the dentition and osteology of the different orders of the Mammalia. As regards the osteological series, he expressed himself in the above-mentioned address of 1881 in the following words :—

"On this head we claim to be somewhat in advance of other museums, on account of the improvements which have been made of late years in preparing and articulating dried skeletons, and in displaying portions of the bony framework in an instructive manner. Formerly all the bones were rigidly fixed together, so that their articular surfaces, if not actually destroyed, were completely concealed, and no bone could possibly be removed and separately examined. The aim of a series of changes in the method of mounting skeletons introduced here, and now adopted, more or less completely, in many other museums, has been to obviate all these difficulties, and to make each bone, as far as possible, independent of all the rest, whilst preserving the general aspect and form of the entire skeleton.

"Another improvement in the osteological series introduced within the last twenty years has been the formation of a special collection designed to show the principal modifications of each individual skeleton throughout the vertebrate classes, by the placing the homologous bones of a number of different animals in juxta-position. For convenience of comparison, the specimens of this series are all placed in corresponding positions, mounted on separate stands, and to each is attached a label bearing the name of the bone and the animal to which it belongs. This series is especially instructive to the students of elementary osteology, and forms an introduction to the general series."

It might have been added with perfect truth that this series of the detached homologous bones of different animals is of equal value and importance to both the palæontologist and the evolutionist ; since with its assistance the former has a ready means of ascertaining the nearest relationships of any fossil bone that may be brought under his notice, while the latter is able to observe the modifications that any particular bone has undergone in different groups of animals. He may notice, for instance, the elongation and slenderness distinctive of the humerus, or arm-bone, of the bat, and contrast it with the short and broad contour characterising the same bone in the mole, while he may observe the elongation of some of the bones of the hind-limbs distinctive of jumping mammals, and their almost total disappearance in the whales and dolphins. If the preparation of this series of specimens (which appears to have been closely connected with his lectures on the osteology of the Mammalia, and their subsequent incorporation in the well-known volume noticed in the sequel) had been the sole limit of the work accomplished by Flower, it would still have been sufficient to entitle him to the gratitude of posterity.

It was while engaged in the development of the collections of this museum that Flower made his important observations on the homologies and mode of succession of the teeth of various groups of mammals, and more especially the marsupials. Here, too, it was that he undertook the investigations which led to his publication of a new scheme of classification for the Carnivora ; and it was likewise during his Conservatorship that he published his valuable series of observations upon the comparative anatomy of the mammalian liver. These and other kindred subjects may, however, better be considered at greater length in a later chapter. It must suffice therefore, to add in this connection that during Flower's term of office the unrivalled series of human skeletons and skulls underwent a very marked and important increase.

By no means the least important part of Flower's work in connection with the museum of the College of Surgeons was the compilation and publication of the first two volumes of the *Catalogue of Osteological Specimens* the first, dealing with man alone, issued in 1879, and the second, written with the aid of his assistant, Dr. J. G. Garson, and treating of the other members of the mammalian class, in 1884. The importance of these works consists in the fact of their being a very great deal more than mere catalogues of the contents of one particular museum. They are, on the contrary, systematic treatises, embodying the views of their chief author on such important subjects as zoological nomenclature and classification, and on the best method of arranging museums which include specimens of the dentition and osteology of both living and extinct animals. They accordingly deserve notice at some considerable length, not only on this account, but as forming a record of the great changes Flower introduced into the museum at this period under his charge.

It appears that the first printed list of the contents of the museum was published in the year 1831. In a few years, however, it became evident that a work of a more ambitious nature was required; and in January 1842, the then Conservator, Professor Owen, presented a report to the Council, on the supreme advantage to be gained by combining in the proposed new Catalogue both the recent and the fossil osteological Catalogues. Acting on this, the Committee of Council resolved that such a Catalogue should be prepared and published, and the duty of doing this was thereupon confided to Mr. Owen.

For some reason or other, this excellent and far-seeing resolution was not acted upon in its entirety ; and although catalogues were in due course compiled by Owen and published, the specimens belonging to animals still extant were entered in volumes. quite distinct from these devoted to fossil bones and teeth ; while the two series of specimens were likewise kept apart in the museum itself. "Hence," as Flower subsequently observed, "each series was incomplete, and required reference to the other for its perfect illustration and comprehension." These defects were remedied during the administration of Flower, who not only arranged the extinct specimens in their proper position among those belonging to recent animals, but likewise followed the same admirable plan in drawing up the Catalogues. Later on, as we shall see in the sequel, he endeavoured to introduce the same scheme into the Natural History Museum, but was prevented by the force of circumstances from carrying his views into full effect, although a small step in the right direction was accomplished.

The first part of the Catalogue of the osteological specimens in the museum of the College which, as already said, is devoted to man alone, is a most laborious, accurate, and valuable work, dealing first with the general osteology of man, then with his dentition, and, thirdly, with the special characters of the osteology and dentition of the different races of the human species— a line of study which had formed the subject of several of his lectures as Hunterian Professor. Nor is this by any means all, for the introduction to this volume forms a valuable compendium of the principles and rules of the science of craniology; the remarks on the mode of measuring skulls, and the method of calculating from such measurements " indices," whereby skulls of different types can be compared with one another with exactness, being models of accuracy and clearness, and rendered the more valuable from the tables by which they are accompanied. For measuring the cubic contents of skulls, Flower was convinced that mustard-seed formed the best and most accurate medium.

In addition to its value as a summary of the contents of that portion of the museum of which it treats, and as a *précis* of its chief author's views at that time as to the classification of mammals, the second part of the Catalogue is of special importance on account of containing an expression of opinion on the subject of zoological nomenclature—a subject on which Flower had previously spoken in no uncertain tones in his Presidential Address to the Zoological section of the British Association at the meeting held in Dublin in 1878, which is republished in *Essays on Museums*.

The keynote of Flower's introduction to his Catalogue was the urgent need of uniformity of nomenclature among zoologists; and on this, and the subject generally, he expressed himself as follows :—

" As there is no matter of such great importance in a

catalogue as the correct naming of the objects described in it, this part of the subject has engaged a very large share of attention in preparing the work. I am not sanguine enough to suppose that the names I have adopted—always after careful research and consideration—will in every case be deemed satisfactory by other zoologists, yet I hope that some advance will have been made towards that most desirable end—a fixed and generally recognised nomenclature of all the best-known species of mammals. Having selected the generic and specific name which I considered most appropriate, I have given the place and date of their first occurrence, but have only admitted such synonyms as have found their way into standard works, judging it better that the remainder should be buried in oblivion, or at all events only retained in professedly bibliographical treatises. In selecting the name chosen, I have been mainly guided by the views which have been gradually gaining general currency among conscientious naturalists of all nations, and which were formulated in what is commonly called the Stricklandian Code, adopted by a Committee of the British Association for the Advancement of Science in 1842, and revised and reprinted by the Association in 1865, and again in 1878. . . . The regulations laid down in these codes for the formation of new names are unimpeachable; and although some of the rules for the selection of names already in existence have given rise to criticism, and are occasionally difficult of practical application when an endeavour is made to enforce them too rapidly, they do in the main, when interpreted with discretion and common-sense, lead to satisfactory results. As what we are aiming at is simply convenience and general accord, and not abstract justice or truth, there are cases in which the rigid law of priority, even if it can be ascertained, requires qualification, as it is certainly not advisable to revive an obsolete or almost unknown name at the expense of one, which if not strictly legitimate, has been universally accepted and become thoroughly incorporated in zoological and anatomical literature; and it is often better to put up with a small error or inconvenience in an existing name than to incur the much larger confusion caused by the introduction of a new one."

These are weighty words of wisdom, and it must be a matter for profound regret to all persons of thoroughly philosophical and well-balanced minds that, by the newer school of naturalists—led by an American section—they have not only been received without the attention they merit as coming from a man of Flower's wide experience and mature judgment, but have been absolutely ignored and the principle they inculcate treated with disdain and contempt. Obscure names, frequently of the most barbarous construction and sound, have been raked up from all conceivable sources and substituted for the well-known terms adopted by Flower and many of his contemporaries; while, to make matters worse, the good old rule that no names antedating the twelfth edition of the *Systema Naturæ* of Linnæus should be recognised in zoological literature has, so far as mammals are concerned, been treated absolutely as a dead letter.

If it be asked what has been the result of thus ignoring the deliberately expressed and matured views of a judicial mind like Flower's, and whether we are perceptibly nearer the attainment of uniformity in the matter of biological nomenclature, the reply must be that the subject is in a more unsatisfactory state than ever, and the desired end as far off. It is perfectly true, indeed, that a section of the students of the systematic side of zoology have agreed among themselves to employ only such names as they believe to be the earliest, quite irrespective of the obscurity of their origin or the rule that such names should be compounded according to classic usage. When, however, we take a broader survey of the field of biology, we find that, almost to a man, the anatomists, the palæontologists, the geologists, the evolutionists, the students of geographical distribution, and other writers who discuss the subject from aspects other than the purely systematic, adhere to the more conservative side in respect of nomenclature. Moreover, even if this were not the case, we should be but little forwarder, seeing that in works like Darwin's *Origin of Species* and Wallace's *Geographical Distribution of Mammals*—which must remain classical so long as zoology lasts as a science—the older style of nomenclature is used. Consequently, even if the proposed emendations and changes were universally adopted, the names employed by these and other contemporary writers would still have to be learnt and committed to memory by all zoological students ; so that, instead of one series of names, as would have been practically the case had Flower's proposal been loyally adopted by his contemporaries and followers, we are compelled to know and remember a double series.

Whether in the end there will not be a reversion to the judicial and temperate conservative compromise proposed by Flower — and almost everything in this world is based more or less upon compromise—from the headstrong and radical mode of procedure followed by some of the younger zoologists, remains to be seen.

Another subject on which Flower insisted very strongly in the work under consideration was the inadvisability of multiplying generic and family divisions in zoology. Here again we may quote his own words.

"I do not mean," he writes, "that with the advancement of knowledge improvements cannot be continually made in the current arrangement of genera. The older groups become so unwieldy by the discovery of new species belonging to them that they must be broken up, if only for the sake of convenience; newly discovered forms which cannot be placed in any of the established genera must have new genera constituted for them, and fuller knowledge of the structure of an animal may necessitate its removal from one genus into another; all these are incidents in the legitimate progress of science. Such alterations should, however, never be made lightly and without a full sense of responsibility for the difficulties which may be occasioned by them, and which often can never be removed. Complete agreement upon this subject can never be expected, as the idea of a *genus*, of an assemblage of animals to which a common generic name may be attached, cannot be defined in words, and only exists in the imagination of the different persons making use of the expression; but there might be no difficulty in coming to some general agreement, if individual zoologists would look at the idea as held by the majority, and would not give way to the impulse to bestow a name wherever there is the slightest opening for doing so."

Here, again, we have golden words, which are unfortunately ignored by a large number of the zoologists and palæontologists of the present day. Most noteworthy, perhaps, in the whole passage, is the emphasis given to the fact that generic groups are but arbitrary creations of the human, and that, far from being natural realities, they are solely and simply formed as matters of convenience, so that their limits are absolutely dependent upon individual or collective opinion.

Consequently, when we hear it said—as we may—that such and such an animal *must* constitute a genus by itself, we may be assured that in nine cases out of ten the speaker is talking nonsense. It *may* do so, but this is purely as a matter of convenience for purposes of classification. As examples of Flower's broad and far-seeing way of looking at the limits of generic groups, we may take his inclusion of the foxes in the same group as the wolves, of the polecats and weasels with the martens, of the two-horned with the one-horned rhinoceroses, and of the blackbirds with the thrushes; and yet in all these instances, as in many others, a large number of his successors—many of whom cannot lay claim to anything approaching his intellectual capacity and his power of separating essentials from trivialities—cannot be content with the grand simplicity of his scheme of classification. What they gain by their involved systems and minute subdivisions is best known to themselves—to the public such complexity tends to render zoology, which ought to be one of the most attractive and delightful of all sciences (and it was one of Flower's endeavours to make it as much so as possible), repulsive and distasteful.

The present writer's opportunities of intercourse with Professor Flower during his tenure of the Conservatorship of the Museum of the College of Surgeons were but few and intermittent, and restricted to the latter part of that time, he may therefore be pardoned for quoting from a biographer who appears to have enjoyed more favourable opportunities in this respect. Before doing so, however, the writer cannot refrain from putting it on record that his own appointment to the Geological Survey of India in the early seventies was largely due to the influence of Professor Flower, who had been his examiner in the Natural Science Tripos at Cambridge, in December 1871.

To revert to the subject of Flower's personality in connection with his appointment in Lincoln's Inn Fields, his biographer in the " Year-Book " of the Royal Society for 1901 writes as follows :—

"His tenure of office, viz., twenty-two years, as Conservator of the museum of the Royal College of Surgeons, was a splendid record of original and laborious work, of great administrative capacity, and of unvarying courtesy to visitors. The museum was most popular under his management. There, amidst the almost unrivalled collections, the tall, fair-haired, and earnest worker was daily to be found, minutely studying, comparing and measuring, or giving directions for the extension, arrangement, and classification of the varied and valuable contents. From a scientific point of view no post could have been better adapted to the man or the man to the post. With many and varied lines of study lying conveniently around him, in the quietude of an office less conspicuous and exacting than the British Museum, in the full vigour of manhood, and in the midst of sympathetic seniors, friends, and assistants, it can well be imagined that Sir William's powers attained great development, and that perhaps he never felt so full of happiness and satisfaction with his original work. It could not well be otherwise. His conscientious devotion to duty, his remarkable skill in devising methods of mounting, his artistic eye, his tact with subordinates, and the esteem in which he was held by zoologists and comparative anatomists at home and abroad, give a clue to his subsequent career, and show the training of one of the most accomplished and courtly comparative anatomists our country has produced."

But there was another side to Flower's work during the greater part of his official connection with the Royal College of Surgeons, and one which brought him into wider and closer contact with the public than was the case with his Conservatorship. This was the delivery of the lectures which form the chief, if not the sole, duty of the Hunterian Professor. According to the statutes of the College, the annual course of lectures, which is short, must be on a different subject each year, but must in all cases be illustrated by preparations in the museum.

The present writer was privileged to attend only one of these courses—on the general structure of the Mammalia—and is therefore not competent to speak from experience of these lectures as a whole. Nevertheless the one course was amply sufficient to convince him of the lecturer's special qualifications for his task. Flower was indeed an ideal lecturer, endowed with a fine presence, a suave and yet penetrating voice, great power of expression, a slow and impressive delivery, and, above all, an absolute mastery of his subject (whatever it might be) down to the minutest and apparently most insignificant details. For him, every detail of structure, whether functional or rudimentary, had a significance and a meaning, and he would never rest satisfied till he had found out what that meaning was, and had laid the whole of the evidence on which he based his conclusions before his audience. That audience, which generally included a considerable number of the elder members of the medical profession, as well as many well-known zoologists and anatomists, invariably listened with rapt attention to the story told so admirably by the accomplished lecturer.

Of these lectures, the first course, delivered in 1870 on the Osteology of the Mammalia, is perhaps the one which has rendered Flower most widely known among zoological students, since, as noticed below, it became the basis of a valuable little volume.

His introductory lecture in February 1870 was largely devoted to the subject of plan, or " type," in Nature, and to the evidence in favour of the transmutation of species and evolution of organised beings—a doctrine which was at that time by no means so widely accepted, even among scientific men, as it is at the present day. In this address the lecturer prefaced his remarks by explaining that since the main part of his anatomical knowledge was derived from the splendid series of specimens and preparations in the museum under his charge, so he intended to act as the mouth-piece of the specimens themselves. After this intro-ductory lecture followed the regular course for the year, which was devoted to the Osteology of the Mammalia, and it is perhaps this series which has rendered the name of Flower most familiar to the ordinary students of scientific zoology and comparative anatomy, since it was published during the same year as a volume in Macmillan's *Manuals for Students*, under the title of *An Introduction to the Osteology of the Mammalia : being the Substance of a Course of Lectures delivered at the Royal College of Surgeons of England.* Such was the success of this admirable little volume— which has ever since formed the recognised text-book on the subject of which it treats, that a second edition was called for in 1876, and a third in 1885. In expand-ing and revising the latter—in which, by the way, the second half of the original title was dropped—the author, owing to the pressure of official duties, called in the assistance of Dr. J. G. Garson, of Cambridge, a well-known zoologist and anatomist.

This book, to be properly appreciated, should be studied in connection with the series of homologous bones of different species of mammals arranged by Flower himself in the museum of the College of Surgeons, to which reference has been made in an earlier part of this chapter, and from which most of the illustrations were drawn. The figures of the dog's skull have been reproduced in a large number of

D

zoological and anatomical works. The plan followed in this volume forms an admirable model for all works of a kindred nature. In the first chapter the author discusses the classification of the mammalia; in the second he describes the skeleton of that group as a whole; while in the remainder the modifications presented by the various bones in the different groups are described in considerable detail. A special feature is the sparing use of technical terms, and the careful explanation of the meaning of those of which the use was unavoidable. Besides being carefully revised and brought up to date, the third edition differed from its predecessors by including a table of the number of vertebræ found in a large series of species.

In the following year (1871) the Hunterian course, which comprised no less than eighteen lectures, was devoted to the functions and modifications of the teeth of mammals, from man to the monotremes, although it was not known at that time that either of the two generic representatives of the latter group really possessed true teeth, the discovery of these organs in the Australian duckbill not having been made till many years later.

Among other subjects included in his Hunterian lectures was the anatomy and affinities of the Cetacea, or whales and dolphins, a group of mammals in which Flower almost from the first displayed a marked and special interest, and on which he became one of the first authorities. Since, however, this is a subject to which fuller reference is made in a later chapter, it need not be further discussed in this place.

In 1872 Flower's Hunterian lectures were devoted to the subject of the digestive organs of mammals; these lectures being reported, with illustrations, in the *Medical Times and Gazette* of the same year.

Perhaps the most important and certainly the most voluminous of these lectures was the series on the "Comparative Anatomy of Man," which extended over several years, the course for 1880 dealing especially with the skulls of the Fiji, Tongan, and Samoan islanders. The subject of anthropology, or the study of the different races of mankind from a zoological stand-point, shared indeed with that of the Cetacea a large part of the Professor's attention, and the two together formed, perhaps, his favourite lines of investigation. In regard to the problems presented by the human race when viewed from this standpoint, Flower has expressed himself as follows :—

"Comparative anatomy is specially occupied in study-ing the differences between one man and another, estimating and classifying their differences, and especi-ally discriminating between such differences as are only individual variations (variations which, when extreme, are relegated to the department of the teratologist) and those that are inherited, and so become characters of different groups and races of the human species. Physical anthropology, moreover, extends its range beyond merely comparing and registering these differ-ences of structure. It also occupies itself with endeavouring to trace their cause, and the circumstances which may occasion their modifications. It endeavours also to form a classification of the different groups of mankind, and so to throw light upon the history and development of the human species."

The races towards which special attention was directed in these lectures were mainly those inhabiting the islands of the Indian Ocean and the Pacific, namely, the diminutive and degraded Andamanese, the Australians, and their near but very distinct neighbours, the Tasmanians, long since extinct, the Melanesians or Oceanic Negroes, and the Polynesians. With the exception of the latter, which the Professor regarded as an aberrant and somewhat mixed modification of the Malay stock, all these different island races were considered to belong to the black or negroid branch of the human species; and it was suggested that the Andamanese were the purest living representatives of a great "Negrito" stock, which had been formerly widely distributed, and had given rise to the true African negroes on the one hand, and to the Oceanic negroes on the other. As regards his view that the aboriginal Australians are members of the negroid branch, it will be pointed out in a later chapter that an alternative opinion has of late years gained considerable favour among anthropologists.

The Hunterian lectures of Flower were, however, by no means restricted to the negro-like races of the islands of the southern oceans. On the contrary, the Professor devoted much attention in the course of the series to the various races to be met with in our Indian dependencies, dwelling especially on the so-called Dravidian (*i.e.* non-Aryan) tribes of the Nilgiris and other districts of southern India, and likewise on the still more remarkable and primitive Veddas of Ceylon.

The Mongols, as typified by the Tatars and Chinese, and their relationship on the one hand to the Eskimo, and thus with the " Indians" of America, and on the other with the Malays, were also discussed at considerable length in these lectures.

The origin of the Egyptians was also a subject to which much attention was devoted by the Hunterian Professor. " The much vexed questions," he said, "who were the Egyptians? and where did they come from? receive no answer from anatomical investigations, beyond the very simple one that they are one of several races which inhabit all the lands surrounding the Mediterranean Sea; that they there lived in their own land far beyond all periods of time measured by historical events, and that in all probability it was there that they gradually developed that marvellous civilisation which has exercised such a powerful influence over the arts, the sciences, and the religion of the whole western world." The truth of these suggestions has been fully confirmed by the subsequent researches of Professor Flinders Petrie.

As a whole, these Hunterian lectures on anthropological subjects were a great success, and won for the Professor increased respect and admiration from scientific men of all classes. They paved the way for the preparation of that invaluable Catalogue of the anthropological specimens in the museum of the College to which allusion has already been made.

When in 1884 Professor Flower, on the resignation of Sir Richard Owen, accepted the Directorship of the Natural History Departments of the British Museum, and was thus compelled to sever his official connection with the Museum of the Royal College of Surgeons, after a service of two-and-twenty years, the following resolution, on the motion of Sir James Paget, seconded by Mr. Erichsen, was unanimously passed by the Council of the College :—

That the Council hereby desire to express to Mr. William Henry Flower their deep regret at his resignation of the office of Conservator. That they thank him for the admirable care, judgment and zeal, with which for twenty-two years he has fulfilled the various and responsible duties of those offices. That they are glad to acknowledge that the great increase of the museum during those years has been very largely due to his exertions, and to the influence which he has exercised, not only on all who have worked with him, but amongst all who have been desirous to promote the progress of Anatomical Science. That they know that while he has increased the value and utility of the museum by enlarging it, by preserving it in perfect order, and by facilitating the study of its contents, he has also maintained the scientific reputation of the College, by the numerous works which have gained for him a distinguished position amongst the naturalists and biologists of the present time. And that, in their placing on record their high appreciation of Mr. Flower, the Council feel sure that they are expressing the opinion of all the Fellows and Members of the College, and that they all will unite with them in wishing him complete success and happiness in the important office to which he has been elected."

This is indeed a splendid, although by no means exaggerated, testimonial to the success of Flower's administration of the Museum of the College˙ of Surgeons, and to the good and lasting work he there effected—work which paved the way to the improvements he was subsequently able to effect in the Natural History Museum.

Note.—On Owen's retirement the post of Superintendent of the Natural History Departments of the British Museum, which he had filled, was merged into the new office of Director ; a wider scope being given to the duties of the post.

CHAPTER III

ON the resignation in 1884 by Sir Richard Owen of the post of Superintendent of the Natural History Departments of the British Museum, which four years previously had been transferred to the magnificent new building in the Cromwell Road, officially known as the British Museum (Natural History), but more commonly designated the Natural History Museum, it was felt by all competent to form an adequate opinion on the subject that Professor Flower was the one man specially and peculiarly fitted for the post. And accordingly, in the course of the year in question, he was duly appointed to that most important and influential position, which may be regarded as conferring upon its occupant the status of the leading official zoologist in the British Empire. It was in this position that Flower became most widely known to the general public ; and here that he received the honours, firstly of C.B., and later on K.C.B., conferred upon him by his Sovereign.

At the date when Sir William (then Professor) assumed the reins of office, the position of Director of the Natural History Museum was of a somewhat anomalous and peculiar nature. At that time (as now) the administration of the museum was divided into four sections, or departments, namely Zoology, Geology (or rather Palæontology), Botany and Mineralogy, each of which was presided over by a " Keeper," who had practically unlimited control, both as regards finance and general arrangement, of his own section. Consequently, as regards these four departments, the Director had very little control over the museum he was nominally supposed to govern; and his functions were to a great extent limited to regulating the " foreign policy " of the institution under his charge, that is to say, its relations to the parent establishment at Bloomsbury, to the Treasury, and to the world at large. In fact, as Sir William once remarked to the present writer, the Director at that time had to find a sphere of work for himself.

Fortunately, such a sphere of work lay ready to hand, and Flower immediately entered upon it with characteristic energy and enthusiasm.

So long ago as the year 1859, Sir Richard Owen, in one of his reports to the Trustees of the Museum, recommended that the new building, in addition to affording ample space for the general series of natural specimens exhibited to the public, should likewise include a hall, or other suitable apartment, for the display of a series of specimens calculated to convey an elementary idea of the general principles of systematic natural history and biological classification to the large proportion of the ordinary public visitor not conversant with that subject. In other words, the feature of the proposed section would be the exhibition of a series of specimens selected to show the more typical characters of the principal groups of organised (and, it was at the time added, crystallised) forms. This, it was urged, would constitute an epitome of natural history, and would convey to the eye, in the easiest and most ready manner, an elementary knowledge of the sciences in question.

In every modification which the plans of the new building underwent, a hall for the purpose indicated in the above passages formed, as Sir William has himself remarked, a prominent feature ; being in the later stages of the development of the building called, for want of a better name, the "Index Museum."

The increasing infirmities of age, coupled with the short time during which he presided over the Natural History collections in their new home, combined, however, to prevent Owen from making any real progress with the so-called Index Museum ; and although he furnished the idea of the scheme and planned the general installation of the hall, the selection and installation of its contents were left to his successor. And, with the vast experience gained by Sir William during his tenure of office in the Royal College of Surgeons, they could not possibly have been left to abler hands.

Here it is necessary to explain that, whether by design or by accident, history sayeth not, the Index Museum and the Central Hall generally were not included in any one of the four great administrative departments of the Museum, so that they consequently came under the immediate and exclusive control of the Director himself.

Nor was Flower long in setting to work at the task which thus lay awaiting his master-hand ; and the Index Museum, as fast as the exigencies of finance and the difficulties of procuring suitable specimens permitted, gradually assumed the shape and character familiar to all visitors of the building, not that in these respects it exactly followed the lines suggested by Owen. In place of being, as was originally proposed, a sort of epitome or index of the main collections in the galleries, it developed rather into something " more like the general introduction preceding the systematic portion of treatises on any branch of natural history."

Whether, in view of this departure from the original conception, Sir William, if starting *de novo*, would have grouped all these separate collections in a single apartment, or whether he would have split them up and placed them at the commencement of the various series in the exhibition galleries to which they respectively pertain, may be a moot point. But, at anyrate, no detriment to his work would ensue if such a splitting-up should be thought desirable in the future. And considerable advantages would undoubtedly result if the series displaying the general morphology and anatomy of the mammals were placed at the entrance of the mammalian gallery, and so on with the other series at present exhibited in the Index Museum.

Be this as it may, the series of specimens and preparations arranged in the Index Museum under the immediate superintendence of Flower is probably unrivalled in its way, and displays in a marked manner that attention to detail and that eye to artistic effect which were among his special attributes. In the " bay " devoted to mammals, special attention was given to the display of specimens illustrating the various forms assumed by the teeth in the different orders and

families, and their mode of succession and replacement;
—subjects in which Flower always displayed special
interest, and in regard to which he made some important
discoveries. Here, too, were exhibited during the latter
half of his tenure of office the skeletons and half models
of a man and a horse, placed in juxtaposition, in order to
display the special adaptations and modifications for,
on the one hand, the upright posture and great brain-
capacity, and, on the other, for the high degree of speed
and endurance essential to an otherwise defenceless
quadruped living, in a wild state, on open plains. In
this exhibit, which forms the frontispiece to his well-
known and deservedly popular little work on *The
Horse*, Sir William always took an especial pride;
and it was one of the first objects to which he directed
the attention of the many illustrious and distinguished
visitors who sought his guidance in viewing the collections under his charge. Another specimen in the same
" bay " of which he was especially proud is the
skeleton of a young chimpanzee, dissected by Dr. Tyson,
and described by that anatomist in a work published
in 1699, under the title of the *Anatomie of a Pigmie*,
being the earliest scientific description of any man-
like ape.

As regards the vertebrate "bays," Sir William
himself (always of course with the aid of trained
assistants) took an active part in the selection and
arrangement of the specimens. In the case of the
invertebrate groups, on the other hand, the task was
left more to his subordinates; while as regards the
botanical section such relegation was, of necessity,
practically complete. Although it has been previously

referred to elsewhere, it may be mentioned that it was during the work on the Index Museum the discovery of the absence in certain groups of birds of the fifth cubital quill-feather was made; a fact now familiar to naturalists under the title of diastaxy, or aquintocubitalism.

A special feature of the vertebrate section of the Index Museum was the attention devoted to the mounting of the skins of the mammals exhibited. In an address delivered to the British Association in 1889, Flower referred to "the sadly neglected art of taxidermy, which continues to fill the cases of most of our museums with wretched and repulsive caricatures of mammals and birds, out of all natural proportions, shrunken here and bloated there, and in attitudes absolutely impossible for the creature to have assumed while alive." And he was determined that the specimens of this nature in the section of the museum under his own immediate superintendence should be the best of their kind, and should serve as models for the renovation of these in the zoological galleries which he had determined to undertake so soon as the opportunity was afforded.

Neither was he less particular in regard to labels describing the exhibits. In the address already referred to, he had written that "above all, the purpose for which each specimen is exhibited, and the main lesson to be derived from it, must be distinctly indicated by the labels affixed, both as headings of the various divisions of the series and to the individual specimens. A well-arranged educational museum has been defined as a collection of instructive labels, illustrated by well-selected specimens." Most, if not all, of the descriptive labels in the vertebrate series of the Index Museum were written by the hand of the Director himself, while all came under his personal supervision before being placed in the museum. Labels of a descriptive nature had hitherto been mainly, if not entirely, conspicuous by their absence on the zoological side of the museum ; and for some time the Index series alone afforded an example of the nature of the Director's views on this all-important subject. Nor was this all ; for in addition to these descriptive labels, other and larger labels were affixed in the cases, bearing the names of the various " classes," " orders," and " families," to which the specimens respectively pertained ; the limits of the space occupied by each group being indicated by black laths, varying in width according to the grade of the group they demarcated. By this means systematic divisions were clearly indicated ; and on no consideration would Flower permit of any single specimen being placed elsewhere than in its proper systematic position.

Another innovation—so far at anyrate as the zoological side of the museum was concerned—was the placing of small maps alongside each specimen or each group, to illustrate, by means of colour, the geographical distribution of the species or group.

As regards the function of the Index Museum, it may be admitted that instead of, as originally intended, serving as an elementary guide in natural history to the uninstructed public, this exhibit is more generally used by serious zoological students, of whom numbers may from time to time be seen, book in hand, and sometimes under the guidance of a teacher, intently poring over the contents of the cases. Such a use—although not perhaps the prime object of a national museum—is, however, at least as important as catering to the requirements of the ordinary visitor.

.The display in systematic and serial order of the external characters and internal anatomy of the leading types of living and extinct animals and plants formed, however, only a part of Flower's scheme of exhibits for the central hall of the museum. Such specimens occupied only the "bays" or alcoves on the west and east sides, and there remained the large central floor space for exhibits of other descriptions. Advantage was taken of this to display examples of the phenomenon of seasonal colour-change in birds, accompanied in some instances, as in the ruff, by the development of special plumes round the neck, or elsewhere; the two species selected for illustration being the aforesaid ruff and the wild duck or mallard; the latter bird, together with many other members of its tribe, being remarkable on account of the assumption by the males at certain seasons of the year of an "eclipse" plumage, almost indistinguishable from that distinctive at all times of the year of the female. Other cases were devoted to showing some of the more remarkable kinds of variation produced from a single wild stock by domestication and artificial selection; the species exhibited for this purpose being several types of the common fowl, the various kinds of pigeons, and the more remarkable strains of the canary. The introduction of domesticated breeds, whose peculiarities are entirely, in the outset at anyrate, the result of man's interference with the ordinary course of Nature, is a notable feature of this portion of the work of Flower, and indicates his sense of the important bearing of such artificial variations on the doctrine of the evolution of organic nature. " Mimicry " by animals of one group of those of another also formed an important part of this introductory series of exhibit; as did likewise the colour-adaptation of animals to their inorganic surroundings. This latter phenomenon is specially illustrated by a series of animals (mammals, birds and reptiles) from the Libyan desert, which are set up amid rocks and sand from the same locality so as to imitate as nearly as possible the natural conditions. And this case, together with one of these to be noticed immediately, affords an excellent example of Sir William's painstaking efforts to make the exhibits in the museum as realistic as possible, and also his influence and per-suasive power in inducing friends or correspondents to aid his endeavours. For in both these instances the animals and their inanimate surroundings were collected on the spot by generous and enthusiastic donors.

The second instance of the adaptation of animals to their surroundings is afforded by the two cases display-ing respectively a summer and a winter scene in Norway, with the birds and mammals in the one in their brown dress, and in the other in their snow-white livery. Since Sir William's death an Arctic fox, in the appro-priate dress, had been added to each case, with a decided improvement to the general effect.

Another exhibit of the above nature is devoted to the phenomenon of albinism and melanism among animals; the two cases in which the specimens are shown containing an extraordinary number of species, varying in size from leopards to mice, in which these remarkable colour-phases are respectively displayed. The admission

E

of such departures from the ordinary type into the museum justifies, it may be mentioned, the introduction of abnormalities of a more startling nature.   Finally, as illustration of a transition from one species towards another, Sir William caused to be set up a series of typical specimens of the common and the hooded crow, together with offspring produced by the union of the two, which are to a great extent intermediate between the parent forms.   In the same cases is a series of gold-finches, showing a complete gradation between birds of different coloration, and commonly regarded as belonging to distinct species.

All the above instances serve to demonstrate, however inadequately, Flower's broad conception of the field to be covered by a national and educational museum, altogether apart from the exhibition of specimens illustrative of systematic natural history.   It is no secret that Sir William wished to add a series illustrative of the present geographical distribution of animals on the surface of the globe; but, for lack of space, all that could be attempted in this direction was the exhibition of the British fauna, together with a map displaying the division of the world into zoological regions, according to the scheme of Messrs. Sclater and Wallace.

For several years, apart from administrative duties, Flower devoted practically the whole of his available time to the elaboration of the Index Museum and the other exhibits in the Central Hall, although he found opportunity to draw up a list of the specimens of Cetacea (whales and dolphins) in the collection of the Museum, which was published by order of the Trustees in 1885.   Probably, indeed, this list was compiled before active work on the Index Museum had commenced. It is a very useful work to the student of the group, although limited to species represented in the Museum collection.

In the autumn of the year 1895 there occurred, however, an event, which may be said to have revolutionised Flower's position in the Museum, and gave him that immediate personal control over the zoological collections which was essential to the full development and perfection of his scheme of museum reform and expansion. At that date Dr. Albert Günther retired from the position of Keeper of the Zoological Department; and it was then resolved by the Trustees of the Museum that this post should be held by Sir William (who, by the way, had been made C.B. in 1887 and K.C.B. in 1892), in conjunction with the office of Director.

This arrangement was continued throughout the remainder of Sir William's term of office, and was likewise renewed when he was succeeded by Professor E. Ray Lankester, the present holder of the combined posts.

This, then, gave Flower, as already stated, the opportunity for which he had so long been waiting; and in January 1896 he undertook the supervision of the reorganisation and rearrangement of the mammal gallery.

Here a digression of some length must be made, in order to make the reader acquainted in a certain degree with the conditions then prevalent in the museum in connection with the galleries open to the public. In the first place, as already indicated, while the skins and bones of recent animals were contained and exhibited in the Zoological Department, the remains

of their extinct relatives, and even the fossilised bones
and teeth of the living species, were relegated to
the Geological Department, which occupies the ground-
floor of the opposite side of the building.   To make
matters worse, the skeletons of living mammals were
exhibited on the second floor of the zoological side of
the building (instead of, as they should have been,
on the ground floor), and thus as far away as they
could possibly be from those of their extinct predecessors.

Such an unnatural and illogical sundering of
kindred objects was altogether repugnant to the mind
of Flower, who in his address to the British Association
in 1889, to which allusion has been already made,
expressed himself as follows :—

"For the perpetuation of the unfortunate separation
of palæontology from biology, which is so clearly a
survival of an ancient condition of scientific culture, and
for the maintenance in its integrity of the heterogeneous
compound of sciences which we now call 'geology,' the
faulty organisation of our museums is in a great measure
responsible.   The more their rearrangement can be made
to overstep and break down the abrupt line of demarca-
tion which is still almost universally drawn between
beings which live now and those which have lived in
past times, so deeply rooted in the popular mind, and so
hard to eradicate even from that of the scientific student,
the better it will be for the progress of sound biological
knowledge."

The force of circumstances, coupled with the expense
which would have been involved, was, however, too
much for even a man with Flower's force of character
and determination, and the attempt to merge the

palæontological with the zoological collections was consequently perforce abandoned.[1] As a compromise a certain number of fossil specimens, or casts of the same, were to be introduced among the recent mammals; while, conversely, a few skeletons of the latter were to take their place among the remains of their extinct forerunners.

In another mooted change, Sir William (as it lay entirely in the Department under his own special control) was, however, more successful. Previously it had been the practice in the museum to separate the skeletons and skulls and horns of mammals from the mounted skins, placing the former in a gallery by themselves, known as the Osteological Gallery. As a result of this, if a visitor wanted to ascertain the peculiarities of the skeleton of any mammal of which the skin was exhibited, he had to mount to the gallery above, and on his arrival there, very probably forgot the essential features of the skin. One of the first resolves in connection with the rearrangement was to do away with the Osteological Gallery altogether, and to place a certain proportion of the skeletons and skulls in juxtaposition with, or near by, the stuffed skins.

Another feature of the old method of exhibition in vogue in the museum was the crowding together of a vast number of specimens, good, bad, and indifferent (mostly either the second or third), many of which were duplicates, in such a manner that the great majority could scarcely be seen at all, while the effect of those that

---

[1] At the cost of a gap in the systematic series, a step has been subsequently made in this direction by the transference of the elephants and sea-cows to the Geological Department.

were more or less visible was marred and obscured by the adjacent specimens. To add to this unsatisfactory state of affairs was the bad condition—due either to age, to bad taxidermy, or both combined—of the bulk of the specimens. Moreover, by some inconceivable Vandalism, dating apparently from a very remote epoch in the museum's history, every specimen was mounted on a stand of polished sycamore, the effect of which was to mar even a first-class specimen of taxidermy. When to the above is added the fact that, beyond the scientific and in most cases also the popular name of the species, nothing in the way of indicating the serial position of the various groups was attempted, while all that was done in the way of descriptive labels was the suspension here and there of frames containing extracts from the "Guide" to the gallery, it may be imagined that the state of the collection was very far indeed behind the Director's idea of what it should be. Moreover, although in the case of the smaller animals a systematic arrangement was followed, the cases containing the larger species were disposed without any reference to the systematic position of the latter.

In regard to such matters the Director had, in the address quoted, already expressed his own views in no uncertain tone, as is evident from the following passage relating to the arrangement of specimens in the public galleries :—

"In the first place," he writes, "their numbers must be strictly limited, according to the nature of the subject illustrated and the space available. None must be placed too high or too low for ready examination. There must be no crowding of specimens one behind another, every one being perfectly and distinctly seen, and with a clear space around it. . . . Every specimen exhibited should be good of its kind, and all available skill and care should be spent upon its preservation and rendering it capable of teaching the lesson it is intended to convey. . . . Every specimen exhibited should have its definite purpose, and no absolute duplicate should on any account be permitted."

The purport of these golden words, which at the time they were written indicated an entirely new departure in museum arrangement and display, was, so far as possible, followed in the rearrangement of the mammal galleries. In the first place, the upper portions of the cases, which were far too high above the ground to permit of the proper exhibition of small specimens, were, except in those containing large mammals, closed up and employed for displaying the labels relating to the larger groups and the maps illustrating their geographical distribution. Then, again, the shelves, in place of being arranged one above another like those in a wardrobe, were reduced in number, and in most instances in width, so as to be suited to the best possible display of the specimens they were intended to carry. Duplicate specimens of all kinds, as well as representatives of species having but little general interest, were relentlessly weeded out and consigned to the store series; while efforts were made to procure new examples, mounted in the best possible manner, of all species—and these were by far the great majority— represented by badly-mounted, or old and faded specimens. This part of the business was found, however, to be a matter which must necessarily occupy much time, as it is impossible to procure examples of rare or large species, in a condition fit for stuffing, at the precise moment when they are required; and there is also the question of expense, which becomes very heavy indeed when renovating and replacing a collection of the proportions of that of the National Museum. This portion of the work has therefore been going on uninterruptedly ever since the first start was made, and is indeed being continued at the present time; for it has been found by experience that a collection of this nature, owing to the terribly bleaching effects of sunlight, requires constant renovation, and that exhibited museum specimens have only a definite and limited period, varying to a considerable extent according to the colour and nature of the hair in individual species, during which they are fitted to be publicly shown. Instead of a museum, when once arranged, being "a joy for ever," it requires constant attention and renovation, so that even, to keep them in proper order, the mammal galleries alone in the Natural History Museum demand a large proportion of the time of one of the officials.

Not the least important of the changes made in the mammalian galleries under the supervision of Sir William Flower was the alteration of the colour of the stands on which the specimens were mounted. These, as already said, were of polished sycamore, the bright reflection from which was exceedingly unbecoming to the specimens, to say nothing of the obvious lack of æsthetic fitness in mounting stuffed mammals upon a polished surface of this nature. Before anything in the way of a change was attempted, Sir William sought the advice of his friend, the late Lord Leighton, after consultation with whom, it was finally decided that in future the stands should be of a good " cigar-colour." This was effected, in the first instance, by scraping and staining the original sycamore stands—a work of great labour and expense; but all new ones were subsequently made of wood more easy to work, walnut being employed in the case of the smaller sizes. Even this improvement, great as it undoubtedly was, did not, however, by any means represent the full extent of the changes in this direction. After a short experience of the aforesaid " cigar-coloured " stands, it was found that the general effect was much improved by gouging out the upper surface of these, with the exception of a narrow rim round the margin, to a depth of a quarter or half an inch, and covering it with a thin layer of sand or earth, upon which leaves, pebbles, etc., might be disposed if required. Instead of " skating on sycamore tables," the animals were by this means shown standing on a very good imitation of a natural land surface.

Nor was this all. At an early period during the rearrangement of the mammal galleries, Sir William suggested that many of the larger species might be mounted upon imitation ground-work covering the entire floor of the cases in which they were exhibited. This idea was forthwith put into execution in several cases, notably in these containing the lions, the tigers, and the group of fur-seals from the Pribiloff Islands, presented by Sir George Baden-Powell. Supposed difficulties with regard to the cleaning of the glass of the cases prevented this plan from being carried out to any greater extent during Sir William's lifetime. But these presumed difficulties were subsequently overcome, and of late years a considerable number of the cases containing the larger species of mammals have been treated in this manner with excellent effect and a vast increase to the general attractiveness of the museum. In some instances a merely conventional ground-work has been introduced, but in others a more realistic effect has been attempted. A notable example of this is the reindeer-case, in which the artificial ground-work is covered with rocks, lichen, moss, and birch-stems obtained from the reindeer pastures of Norway. Similarly, the Arctic musk-oxen have been placed on an imitation snow-slope. Although, as already said, much of this work has been carried out since his death, the idea originated entirely with Flower. A similar grouping of animals on artificial ground-work—when possible in imitation of the natural surroundings—has been instituted in some of the American museums, but whether following Flower's lead, or as an original inspiration, I am unable to say.

At the time when Sir William took over the office of Keeper of the Zoological Department (in addition to the Directorship), the scheme then in vogue at the museum scarcely assigned to man his real zoological position —at the head of the order Primates in the mammalian class. It is true that in the osteological gallery the genus Homo was represented by a couple of skeletons and a series of skulls. But in the gallery devoted to stuffed specimens man, as an integral portion of the exhibited series, was conspicuous by his absence. This by no means suited the views of the Director, who in an obituary notice of Owen quoted with approval a statement of the great anatomist to the effect that no collection of zoology could in any way be regarded as complete without a large amount of space being devoted to the display of the physical characteristics of the various races of the human species. "The series of zoology would lack its most important feature were the illustrations of the physical characters of the human race omitted." Such a series, thought Owen in 1862, would require a gallery of something like 150 feet in length, by 50 feet in width, for its proper display. Stuffed specimens being, of course, out of the question, the series was to include "casts of the entire body, coloured after life, of characteristic parts, as the head and face, skeletons of every variety arranged side by side for facility of comparison, the hair preserved in spirit, showing its characteristic sign and distinctive structures, etc." Had photography been in anything like its present advanced position in 1862, no doubt its aid would have been claimed in illustrating the various racial types of the human species.

A gallery of anything like the dimensions required by Owen was quite out of the question when Flower planned the addition of an anthropological section to the mammalian series, but one-half of the portion of the upper mammal gallery now open to the public was reserved for this purpose, so that man took his proper place in the zoological series immediately after the gorilla, chimpanzee, and the other man-like apes, which, in their turn, were preceded by the lower types of monkey. In the main, the specimens exhibited in this series follow on the lines suggested by Owen, including coloured casts of the upper part of the body, or the head and neck alone, specimens of the hair, skulls, skeletons, etc.

In addition to these is a series of photographs of heads enlarged to natural size, and including, whenever possible, a full face and a profile view of each individual represented. Flower took great interest in these photographs (as in the anthropological series generally), and made several experiments before finally deciding as to the scale to which they were to be enlarged. As facilities for photographing in the museum itself were at the time very limited, Flower enlisted the assistance of Dr. H. O. Forbes, Director of the Liverpool Museums, who entered enthusiastically into the project, and under whose superintendence the great majority of the reproductions from photographs now exhibited was produced; the arrangement being that Liverpool should have a copy of every photograph forwarded for reproduction.

The races of mankind were arranged in the gallery according to Flower's own scheme, fuller reference to which is made elsewhere in the present volume. Flower himself did not survive long enough to see the arrangement he had plotted out fully installed. Of late years, although some progress has been made in this direction, the series of coloured casts of the various human races has not increased so rapidly as Flower had hoped they would; but, nevertheless, a fairly representative series had been brought together, and there is, at present, ample space for additions when opportunities of acquiring new specimens occur. It should be added that Flower inaugurated the plan of making a collection of photographs of the various human races to be kept in the study series.

It must not, however, be supposed that Flower, during his too brief tenure of the office of Keeper of the Zoological Department, by any means confined his attention to the mammalian galleries. On the contrary, he had with his own hands rearranged two of the cases in the bird gallery, namely, those containing the humming-birds and the woodpeckers ; and shortly before his resignation he was planning the rearrangement of all the cases in this section ; a work which since his death has been carried out to completion on the same lines. In this connection it is, however, only fair to state that in the obituary notice of Flower, published in the " Year-Book " of the Royal Society for 1901, full justice has not been done to his predecessors. The passage in question runs as follows :—

"Every effort was made to give the specimens natural postures and natural surroundings. Thus, for example, the tree on which the woodpecker was at work, was cut down, the foliage modelled in wax, and all the surroundings carefully kept. Hovering birds were suspended by fine wire or thread. Birds making nests in holes, such as the Manx shearwater, sand-martin and kingfishers, either had the actual parts or a model of these beside them, just as the nests of the gannets and guillemots on the Bass Rock were shown with their natural environment."

The obvious inference from this would be that the cases of birds mounted in imitation of their natural environment, inclusive of the splendid model of a portion of the Bass Rock, with its feathered inhabitants placed

in the "pavilion" at the end of the bird gallery, are due
to the initiation of Flower. This is far from being the
case; and he himself would have been the very last
man to claim credit which was not his due. As a
matter of fact, the idea of mounting birds in this manner
originated with Dr. Bowdler Sharpe during the Keepership of Dr. Günther; the first case installed on these
lines being the one containing the common coot. The
series was continued during Dr. Günther's term of office,
and was kept up by Flower after his succession to the
Keepership. As regards the Bass Rock model, this was
also installed during Dr. Günther's Keepership, and, I
believe, while Owen was Superintendent. What Flower
did initiate in the bird gallery was the rearrangement of
the wall-cases on much the same lines as the mammal
galleries, including the rejection of duplicates and
uninteresting species, and the replacement of worn-out
and badly-mounted specimens, by new and artistically
set-up examples, and the addition of maps and descriptive labels. As a matter of fact, the replacement and
remounting of specimens have been carried out to a
much greater extent among the birds than has been
found possible with the mammals. A large number of
the birds have been mounted by Cullingford of Durham,
whereas nearly all the mammals have been set up by
three London taxidermists, namely Rowland Ward,
Ltd., Gerrard, and Pickhardt. This plan of employing
several firms of taxidermists, instead of giving all the
work to one, was much favoured by Flower, as it
gave rise to a healthy competition and rivalry, and
thus produced better results; the different firms
being kept up to the mark by having their names affixed

to the more important examples of their respective work.

Before his last illness Flower had in contemplation a plan for treating the reptile and fish galleries (in which the crowded exhibits displayed a monotonous and dismal " khaki " hue) on the above lines, but this work was left for his successor, by whom it is in course of being carried out with characteristic energy and originality.

There is, however, another section of the zoological department of the museum which owes its conception entirely to Sir William Flower, and which he was fortunately spared to complete. This is the whale-room, or whale-annexe, as it might be better called; for it is a temporary structure of galvanised iron, lined with match-boarding built out from the north-west angle of the building, and entered by a passage leading out of the corridor alongside the bird gallery. At the time that Flower took over the Keepership of the Zoological Department, with the exception of a skeleton of the sperm-whale, placed in the middle of the Central Hall, the specimens of Cetacea were housed in a portion of the basement, never intended for a public gallery and very unsuited to that purpose. The collection consisted mainly of skeletons and skulls, together with samples of whalebone and teeth; for it had been found by experience that it was a practical impossibility to mount the skins of the larger whales for exhibition purposes. Indeed, there is great difficulty in doing this even in the case of the dolphins, porpoises, and smaller whales, owing to the fact that their skins are saturated with oil, which, even after the most careful preparation, is almost sure, sooner or later, to exude through the pores, and render the specimens unsightly, if not absolutely unfit for exhibition.

Previously to Flower's attempt to make an adequate and striking exhibition of the bodily form of the larger whales, some of the smaller members of the group, such as the killer-whale, had been modelled in America in papier-maché; one such model of the species in question being exhibited in the museum. Flower, however, conceived the idea of making models in plaster of even the largest species of whales; but, in order to save both material and space, resolved that these should be restricted to one-half of the animal, and should be constructed upon the actual skeleton, thereby ensuring, with the aid, when possible, of measurements taken from carcases, practically absolute accuracy as regards size and proportion. In due course, after great labour and care, such half-models were built up on the skeletons of the sperm-whale, the southern right-whale, and two species of fin-whale, or rorqual, while others were made of some of the smaller kinds, such as the narwhal and the beluga or white whale. Skeletons and skulls of other species, together with complete models or stuffed skins, or models of the head alone, of many of the porpoises and dolphins, and other specimens illustrating the natural history of the Cetacea, were likewise placed in the new annexe, which was opened to the public on Whit Monday 1897. Flower had always been impressed with the great structural difference between the toothed whales, as represented by the sperm-whale, grampuses, porpoises, dolphins, etc., on the one hand, and the whalebone whales, such as the right-whales, humpbacks, and finners, on the other; and in order to emphasise this essential distinction, he caused the skeletons and models of the one group to be mounted with their heads in one direction, while those of the second were turned the opposite way.

Although it was found impossible to obtain a skeleton of the Greenland right-whale, Flower was able to persuade Captain Gray, a well-known whaler, to carve a miniature model in wood, which gives an excellent idea of the proportions, especially the huge size of the head and mouth, of this interesting species. Sketches on the walls of the building illustrate the habits and mode of capture of the sperm-whale, while others serve to show the bodily form of species not yet represented by models.

At the time it was opened this exhibit was absolutely unique; and, in the belief of the writer, it remains so to the present day. Unfortunately, the size and design of the building, which has a row of wooden posts down the middle, are such as greatly to interfere with the proper effect of the specimens exhibited; and it is much to be hoped that means will be found to erect a larger gallery, of a more permanent nature, which will not only allow the contents of the present structure to be adequately seen, but will likewise leave space to permit of models of other species, such as the humpback whale, to be added to the series.

Hitherto I have dwelt exclusively upon Sir William's efforts to improve the museum under his charge, from the point of view of the general public, that is to say, as an institution for the exhibition of natural history specimens. It must, however, be always remembered that

F

this was but one side of his task, and that he laboured hard during the whole time of his official connection with the museum not only to increase the study, or reserve, collections (which are those on which the real scientific work of the museum is almost exclusively based), but to add to the space available for their storage and for the workers by whom they are studied.

Early in his career as Director he recognised the insufficiency of the accommodation of this nature, although, as usual, he expressed his opinion in extremely cautious and guarded language. For instance, in his address as President of the Museum Associations in 1893, after referring to the deficiencies of all, at that time, modern museums, which were described as having been built during a period when opinion was still divided as to the proper function of institutions of this nature, he continued as follows :—

"In none, perhaps, is this more strikingly shown than in our own—built, unfortunately, before any of the others, and so without the advantages of the experience that might have been gained from their successes or their shortcomings. Though a building of acknowledged architectural beauty, and with some excellent features, it cannot be taken structurally as a model museum when the test of adaptation to the purpose to which it is devoted is rigidly applied."

This unsuitableness, it may be added, is apparent not only in the lack of accommodation for the study series, but in the exhibition galleries themselves, where architectural ornament interferes with the proper display of the specimens, if indeed it does not absolutely preclude their being placed on the walls, while an excess of light (which has been partially remedied by blocking up the lower portion of the windows in some of the zoological galleries) causes the specimens to become prematurely bleached and faded.

As regards the deficiency of accommodation for the study series in the museum, Sir William endeavoured to remedy this, so far as possible, by closing some portions of the galleries previously open to the public—a step, which, however necessary, tended to mar the building, so far as exhibition purposes are concerned.

"While thus maintaining," writes his biographer in the "Year-book" of the Royal Society for 1901, "the high scientific reputation of the great National Museum, he continued to popularise the institution and science by taking parties of working men round the museum on Sundays, and occasionally a distinguished visitor, like Dr. Nansen, would also join the group. Nor was he less attentive to members of the Royal Family, or to distinguished statesmen, like Mr. Gladstone, who honoured the museum with their presence. Foreign rulers, like the Queen of Holland, the Prince of Naples, the Empress Frederick of Germany, and the King of Siam, were also interested in the collection, so that the popularity and welfare of the museum were greatly extended by the Director's tact and urbanity. Formerly, he had taken a leading part in interesting the Prince of Wales (his present Majesty), who was present at Sir James Paget's Hunterian Oration in 1877, in the Museum of the Royal College of Surgeons, and in arranging for an exhibition of the Prince's hunting trophies at the Zoological Society shortly afterwards, so in his new sphere royal and other powerful influences were utilised for the improvement and popularising of the collection."

King Edward, as Prince of Wales, it may be added, was a constant attendant at the meetings of the Board of Trustees at the Museum during Sir William Flower's administration; and would occasionally, at the close of the meeting, accompanied by the Director, make an inspection of some of the galleries. As indicative of the interest he took in the details of the arrangement of the museum, it may be mentioned that on one of these tours of inspection His Majesty took exception to the position assigned to the head of a reindeer, and desired that it might be placed elsewhere.

One other point in connection with Sir William's administration may be noticed. Ever since its establishment the hall and public exhibition galleries of the Natural History Museum had been guarded during exhibition hours by members of the Metropolitan Police—an arrangement which involved a very large expense to the country. Flower suggested that, provided two or three police sergeants and constables were detailed for special duty, the general work of guarding the collections could be equally well done by members of the Corps of Commissionaires, thereby not only effecting a considerable financial saving, but likewise a fresh area of employment for a very deserving class of the community. This arrangement, which was found to work smoothly and satisfactorily, has remained in force ever since. It may be added that the opening of the museum for a limited number of hours on Sunday afternoons commenced during Flower's tenure of office;

this arrangement being common to other institutions of a like nature.

At the special recommendation of the Trustees, the Treasury, when Sir William reached the age for retirement, according to Civil Service rules, extended his term of office for three years. A lengthened period of physical weakness and prostration rendered it, however, impossible for Flower to avail himself of the whole of this extension, and in July 1898 the state of his health was such that he felt himself compelled to send in his resignation.

When this resignation was accepted by the Standing Committee of the Trustees of the Museum, a special Minute, signed by Lord Dillon, gave expression to the regret felt by that body and the Trustees generally at the retirement of Sir William, to whom every compliment was paid as a worthy successor of Sir Richard Owen, and as one who had done so much towards the re-organisation of a museum pre-eminent amongst institutions of its kind.

To enter upon the relations of Flower to his subordinates in the Museum is treading upon somewhat delicate ground; it may be safely affirmed, however, that to those who were in full sympathy and accord with his way of looking at things and his schemes for the general advancement and improvement of the institution under his charge, no truer friend or kinder master could possibly have been found. Owing to the fact that the time of the permanent officials of the museum is for the most part fully occupied in working out the store collections, and registering and, when necessary, describing new acquisitions, Sir William soon found that he had not sufficient skilled labour at his disposal wherewith to carry out the installation of the Index Museum and his meditated improvements in the exhibition series. Accordingly he obtained the assent of the Treasury to employ the services of a few scientific men not on the staff of the museum for these purposes; an arrangement which has been continued under his successor.

Sir William's services to the museum, as well as to science in general, are commemorated by a bust, executed by Mr. T. Brock, and placed on the south side of the entrance to the first " bay " of the Index Museum. The funds necessary for this were raised by the " Flower Memorial Committee," to which Mr. F. E. Beddard, Prosector of the Zoological Society, acted as Secretary. The bust, which in a profile view, is an excellent likeness of the late Director, was unveiled on 26th July 1903, by the Archbishop of Canterbury, in the presence of a representative assemblage of men of science and personal friends, as well as of statesmen.

The proceedings were opened by Professor E. Ray Lankester, the Director of the Museum, who moved that Lord Avebury (better known in scientific circles as Sir John Lubbock), the Chairman of the Memorial Committee, should take the chair. The Chairman, having taken his seat, expressed his pleasure in being called upon to preside at the ceremony, on account of his admiration and respect for the late Sir William Flower, and for the services he had rendered to zoological science.

Dr. Philip Lutley Sclater, the Secretary of the Zoological Society, also spoke as an old and intimate friend of the late Director, with whom he had been brought into specially close contact during the long period the latter presided over the Zoological Society.

The Archbishop of Canterbury, in a brief speech previous to unveiling the bust, referred to two traits in Flower's character which had specially struck his Grace, and which were seldom found associated in the same individual, one of these being his great love of talking on his own special subjects of study, and the other that, in spite of this, he never bored even the least interested of his hearers. During his Directorship Flower had done more to popularise the museum, and museums generally, than had any other man of science.

The proceedings closed with the usual vote of thanks to the Chairman.

In addition to writing numerous scientific memoirs, Flower found time during his tenure of the Directorship of the museum to prepare for publication two volumes of considerable interest. The first was the one on *The Horse*, issued in 1891, to which fuller reference is made in a later chapter; and the second, the well-known *Essays on Museums*, which appeared in 1898, and consists of a collected series of essays, articles, addresses, etc., on natural history and kindred subjects. A melancholy interest attached to this volume (which is dedicated to Lady Flower), since, as we are told in the preface, it was compiled during a period of enforced restraint from active occupation, which was evidently only the prelude to the final breakdown.

It was also during his Directorship of the Museum that *The Study of Mammals* saw the light.

CHAPTER IV

AS PRESIDENT OF THE ZOOLOGICAL SOCIETY
[1879-1899]

DURING a portion of his tenure of office as Conservator of the Museum of the Royal College of Surgeons, and throughout the whole of his Directorship of the Natural History Museum, Sir William Flower occupied the Presidential Chair of the Zoological Society of London— the oldest body of its kind in existence. The events narrated in the present chapter occurred therefore during the period covered by its two immediate predecessors; nevertheless, this method of treatment, although breaking the chronological order, has been found, on the whole, the most convenient.

The Zoological Society, it may be observed, has been in the habit of selecting its presidents from three distinct classes. As in the case of the late Prince Consort, the president may be a personage of exalted rank without any claim to a special knowledge of zoology. . On the other hand, as exemplified by the Earl of Derby, who filled the office in the " fifties," the Marquis of Tweeddale in the " seventies," and the Duke of Bedford at the present time, he may combine high rank with a more or less pronounced taste for and knowledge of natural history, or, finally, as in the case of the founder, Sir Stamford Raffles, he may be selected solely for his eminence as a zoologist or as a lover of animals.

On the death of the Marquis of Tweeddale, 29th December 1878, Professor Flower was selected by the Council to fill the presidential chair; the appointment being duly ratified at the Annual Meeting of the Society held the following spring. From that date till the year of his death, Flower was annually re-elected president by the unanimous vote of the meeting. He made an admirable president, his deliberate mode of speaking being specially well adapted to the comments expected from a scientific man occupying the presidential chair at the scientific meetings. From his wide knowledge of zoology, anatomy, and palæontology, he was able to speak to the point on almost all the papers read at the Society's meetings; and those privileged to listen to his remarks on any specimen in which he was specially interested will not readily forget the impressive manner in which he brought its more salient and characteristic features to the notice of his hearers. Many of his more important scientific memoirs communicated to the Society had been published in its *Proceedings* or *Transactions*, before he accepted the presidential chair, in days when the calls on his time were not so pressing or so numerous as they afterwards became; but even after his elevation to the presidency several valuable memoirs were received from him, the most important being, perhaps, one on the classification and affinities of the dolphins, to which fuller reference is made in another chapter.

During Flower's presidency several important events and changes occurred in the affairs of the Zoological

Society; and although the management was to a very great extent in the hands of the Secretary, Dr. P. L. Sclater, yet in matters of extreme importance the influence and opinions of the president always made themselves felt—the more so, perhaps, that they were not in special evidence in the case of trivial matters.   In the early eighties the Society suffered severely from financial depression, its income in the years 1883 and 1884 falling far below its expenditure.   Thanks, however, to the patient sagacity and great administrative powers of the president and secretary, the affairs of the Society were soon put on a much more satisfactory basis, and long before the death of the former, a state of prosperity was reached which had seldom, if ever, been equalled, and certainly never excelled.

In the first year of his presidency, Flower delivered one of the Davis lectures in the Society's Gardens, the subject being birds that do not fly, and he also lectured in the two following years, selecting as his subjects in 1881 firstly whales, and secondly dolphins.   The following year was notable on account of the sale to the great American showman, Barnum, of the African elephant " Jumbo."   The reason for thus parting with a valuable and interesting animal was that it was unsafe to keep it in the gardens any longer.   The sale, as stated in the " Record" of the Society, caused a good deal of public excitement, but the Council would not have parted with the animal unless satisfactory reasons for so doing had been laid before it by the responsible Executive of the Gardens.

A still more important event occurred in 1883, namely the transference of the Society's Offices and Library from

No 11 to No 3 Hanover Square ; the freehold of the
latter house having been secured by the Council at a cost
of £16,250. Such an important transaction would not,
we may be assured, have been allowed to take place
without the most careful deliberation and consideration
on the part of the President.

On the first meeting of the Society, held on 1st April
1884, in its new premises, the President took the
opportunity of congratulating the Fellows present on
the very great improvement in the Meeting-room, the
Library, and the Offices, resulting from the change. The
Society had occupied the old house, No 11 Hanover
Square, for forty-one years, and had long since quite
outgrown the accommodation it afforded in all the three
departments mentioned above.

The income of the Society had increased from £9137
in 1843 to £28,966 in 1883, with a corresponding
increase of clerical work. The Library had been almost
entirely formed since the earlier of these dates, and
was rapidly increasing, and the attendance of the
Fellows at the evening meetings for scientific business
had been such that the old rooms were quite inadequate
for their accommodation. The President trusted that
the increased facilities afforded by the move would be
taken advantage of by the Fellows in promoting, with
even greater zeal than previously, the work for which
the Society was founded, and in maintaining and extending the high reputation it had acquired in the scientific
world.

Few presidents or chairmen, whether of scientific
societies or of commercial companies, could have had a
more satisfactory record of progress to lay before their

supporters. The following account of certain events in the Society's history which took place in 1887 is extracted from the " Record " of its work :—

" In order to mark the Jubilee of her late Majesty Queen Victoria which took place this year, in some special way, it was decided to hold the General Meeting in June in the Gardens. After the usual formal business had been transacted, the Silver Medal awarded to the Maharaja of Kuch-Behar was presented to His Highness in person, and suitably acknowledged. Professor Flower, C.B., President of the Society, then delivered an address, which was printed as an Appendix to the Council's Report. It dealt in general terms with the principal points in the history of the Society, from its foundation in 1826, tracing its progress throughout. The connection of the Royal Family with the Society as Patrons and Donors, the scientific meetings, the publications, the Davis Lectures, the menagerie, and the recent improvements in the Gardens were passed in review. The President concluded by appealing for the continued support of the public, either by becoming Fellows or by visiting the Gardens, and expressed the hope that the ' brief record of the Society's history would show that such support was not undeserved by those who have had the management of its affairs.' A reception held after the meeting was numerously attended by the Fellows and their friends, and by many specially invited guests, among whom were the Queen of Hawaii and Princess Liliokalani, the Thakor Sahib of Limdli, H.H. the Prince Devawongse, and the Maharaja of Bhurtpore."

The reception, which was held on 15th June in brilliant weather, was a marked success; the number of foreign visitors in their native dresses lending additional patches of colour to the scene. The President's address on the occasion is reprinted in his *Essays on Museums*.

Referring to Sir William's death, the "Record" of the Society has the following paragraph :—

"On 1st July [1899] the Presidentship of the Society became vacant by the death of Sir William Flower who had filled the office for more than twenty years. During this period Sir William Flower had regularly occupied the Presidential chair, and had been constantly engaged on committees and on other matters connected with the Society's affairs. In Sir William Flower the Society lost a zoologist of the highest ability and a most able and energetic President. To succeed him the Council selected His Grace the Duke of Bedford as President, and their choice was confirmed at the Anniversary Meeting in 1900."

CHAPTER V

In the course of the preceding chapters numerous more or less incidental references have been made to the contributions of Sir William Flower to biological literature, as well as to his many improvements in museum organisation and arrangement. The more detailed discussion of these has, however, been reserved for the present and succeeding chapters, of which the first two are devoted to the zoological and the third to the anthropological side of his work, while in the fourth his views in regard to museums and certain other subjects are taken into consideration.

Regarding the general scientific work of Flower, it must be confessed at the outset that this is characterised in the main by its conscientious carefulness and exactness, rather than by brilliancy of thought, conception, or style. Great attention to detail, both as regards the work itself and in reference to authorities (which were always most carefully verified), is indeed one of the leading features of his labours; but there is no epoch-making discovery or comprehensive generalisation which can be associated with his name. In connection with his careful attention to small and apparently trivial points of detail, the following passage from Professor Ray

95

Lankester's obituary notice in *Nature* may be appropriately quoted :—

" He did his own work with his own hands, and I have the best reason to know that he was so deeply shocked and distressed by the inaccuracy which unfortunately crept into some of the work of his distinguished predecessor, Owen, through the employment of dissectors and draughtsmen, whose work he did not sufficiently supervise, that he himself determined to be exceptionally careful and accurate in his own records and notes."

In another passage of his notice the same writer observes that :—

" Caution and reticence in generalisation certainly distinguish all Flower's scientific writings. Whilst he was on this account necessarily not known as the author of stirring hypotheses, his statements of fact gained in weight by his reputation for judgment and accuracy."

Flower's zoological studies related entirely to the vertebrates and almost exclusively to mammals, although he devoted a few papers, such as the one on the gular pouch of the great bustard, and that on the skull of a cassowary, to birds. Other groups, I believe, he never touched. In the earlier years of his scientific career, at anyrate, his labours were in the main devoted to the anatomical aspect of zoology, such subjects as the dentition, osteology, and the structure and characters of the brain and viscera claiming a much larger share of his attention than was bestowed on the myology. In latter years the classification of the major groups of the mammalia received much attention from Flower. Not that he was in any way what is nowadays called a systematist in zoology, that is to say, he took no active part in describing new species (not to mention sub-species, which had scarcely begun to be recognised by naturalists in his day), or the redefining of generic groups, and other work of this nature. Indeed, as mentioned in the chapter devoted to his career at the College of Surgeons, he was extremely conservative in this respect, and strongly opposed to the modern fondness for small generic groups, and also for changing generic names which, from long association, have come almost to be regarded as household words and integral parts of the English language. The substitution of the name *Procavia*, for *Hyrax*, the familiar title of the Klip-dass, was, for instance, very repugnant to him, although loyally accepted when found to be coming into general use.

As a matter of fact, so far as my information goes, with the exception of certain whales and dolphins, and one extinct sea-cow (*Halitherium*), Flower never named a new species of animal, nor, I think, did he ever propose a new generic term. Indeed, so opposed was he to any interference with names of the latter description in general use, that when several such were replaced by alternative ones in the *Study of Mammals*, it was expressly stipulated by him that the responsibility for such substitution should rest solely with the present writer.[1]

The modern system of forming trinomials to indicate the local races, or sub-species, of mammals (as exemplified by *Giraffa camelopardalis rothschildi* and *Giraffa camelopardalis capensis* for two of the local phases of

[1] An American writer has recently attributed, quite unjustifiably, the names in question to Flower.

G

the species of giraffe typified by *G. camelopardalis* of the Egyptian Sudan and Abyssinia), was practically in its infancy during the active life-time of Flower, and it is doubtful how he would have approved of the extent to which it has been subsequently carried. Nevertheless, that he appreciated the practice of recognising minute local differences of colour, size, etc., in the same species of mammals is evident from an incident within the writer's own knowledge, which occurred at the Natural History Museum, when a tray containing the local phases of one of the species of the small squirrel-like rodents known as chipmunks was submitted to his notice; his remark being that such variations from a common type ought in nowise to be ignored, if we wished to make our knowledge of animals anything like complete, and that the simplest way of indicating such differences was to assign them distinct names.

In a general way, however, it may be said that Sir William's sympathies were with the wider and more philosophical aspects of zoology rather than with the details of specific and sub-specific distinction (which, by the way, have scarcely any more right to be regarded as real philosophical science than has stamp-collecting) [1]; and that, from a systematic standpoint, his interest was very largely concentrated on the relationships existing between the mammals of to-day and their extinct predecessors. Several of his lectures and papers, and one especially of his separate works (that on *The Horse*) were indeed devoted to this aspect of the subject; and

[1] The present writer has the less compunction in making this assertion, seeing that he himself is responsible for naming no inconsiderable number of these so-called sub-species of mammals.

on every possible occasion he emphasised his conviction of the necessity of studying (and arranging in museums) living and extinct mammals together, if we wish to make our science really practical.

As a matter of fact he had the strongest possible objection to the recognition of " palæontology " as a science apart from zoology, and he even went so far as to mildly rebuke (in his own inimitably courteous and gentle manner) the present writer, for venturing to offer to the public a volume on that subject. To a great extent, no doubt, he was perfectly right in this contention, although there are points of view from which " palæontological " works are decidedly convenient, even if their existence and production cannot be logically justified.

As regards the particular groups of mammals (other than man) in which Flower was more especially interested, there can be no doubt that the Cetacea (whales and dolphins) occupied the first position. And on this subject he was undoubtedly one of the first authorities, his only possible rivals in this country, at anyrate, being Sir William Turner and Professor Struthers. Next to this group came, perhaps, the marsupials, in which a most important discovery was made by Flower in regard to the succession and replacement of the teeth.

Not even the most sympathetic of biographers would attempt for one instant to assume that his hero—if a zoologist—could by any possibility be infallible; and it has to be recorded that many changes and amendments have had to be made in Flower's conclusions. Perhaps, indeed, Sir William has been to some extent especially unfortunate in this respect, owing to the extreme imperfection of the state of our palæontological (I must use the objectionable word) knowledge at the date when much of his best work was accomplished. At that time, in spite of the enormous and valuable results achieved by Cuvier, Owen, and others, mammalian palæontology may be said to have been in its infancy compared to its present state; the wonderful discoveries in North and South America being then either unknown or only partially revealed, and the same being the case with regard to those made known by the working of the phosphorite beds in Central France.

These and other discoveries have, for instance, totally revolutionised our ideas with regard to the affinities of the different families of the modern Carnivora, and have thus led to considerable modifications of the views entertained by Flower as to the relationships of the members of this group.

Moreover, there is another important factor which has to be taken into consideration. At the time when Sir William wrote his celebrated memoir on the Carnivora, the effects of what is now universally known among zoologists as " parallelism in development" were quite unrecognised. By " parallelism " (to abbreviate the expression) is meant, it may be explained, a remarkable tendency which undoubtedly exists among animals of markedly diverse origin to become more or less like one another in at least one important structural feature, when living under similar physical conditions, or specially adapted for similar modes of existence. Not unfrequently this structural resemblance, when closely examined, is found to be less close than might at first sight have seemed to be the case; the adaptation having been

brought about by the modification of structures originally more or less dissimilar towards a common type.
In other words, the same goal has been reached by two
different routes.

An excellent example of this is offered by the development of " cannon-bones " in the lower portion of
the limbs of the members of the horse tribe on the one
hand and those of the deer and antelopes on the other ;
the object of this lengthening and strengthening of this
part of the limb being in both instances the attainment of
increased speed. Whereas, however in the one instance
the cannon-bone is formed from one original element,
in the other it is the result of the fusion of two such
elements. In this case, indeed, the difference in the
structure of this part of the skeleton in the two groups
is so apparent as to leave no reasonable doubt as to the
remoteness of the affinity between their respective
ancestors. There is, however, a certain group of extinct South American hoofed mammals in which the
cannon-bone corresponds exactly in origin and structure
with that of the horse, from which it might be assumed
that the two animals were closely related, whereas, from
other evidence, we know that they are widely sundered.
Approximately similar structures are therefore in many
instances far from being indications of genetic affinity
between the animals in which they respectively occur.
Before the occurrence of this parallelism was recognised
by naturalists as an important factor in their development, such resemblances were, however, frequently
regarded as indications of a common parentage, so that
animals which had comparatively little to do with one
another were brigaded as members of the same assemblage.

With these preliminary remarks, we may proceed to a general survey of Sir William's zoological work. It has, however, been found convenient to relegate the consideration of his numerous memoirs on the Cetacea to the next chapter, by which means their connection will be made more apparent than if they were discussed among those on other sections of zoology.

The first zoological paper (and indeed the first scientific work of any description) published by Flower seems to have been that on the dissection of one of the African lemurs belonging to the genus *Galago*, which appeared in the Zoological Society's *Proceedings* for 1852, and serves to prove, as mentioned in the first chapter, that the author was at that time holding the post of Curator of the Museum of the Middlesex Hospital. The paper itself is of little importance, dealing only with the structure of the muscles and viscera of the species in question.

The next paper on the list, which appeared in the same journal for 1860, was also written during this part of Flower's career; it is one of the few devoted to the anatomy of birds, and describes the gizzard of the Nicobar pigeon and other graminivorous species.

About this time Flower began to devote his attention to the mammalian brain; his first contribution on this subject being " Observations on the Posterior Lobes of the Cerebrum of the Quadrumana, with the Description of the Brain of a *Galago*," of which an abstract appeared in the *Proceedings* of the Royal Society of London for 1860, although the complete memoir was not published till 1862, in the *Philosophical Transactions*. The date of publication of the abstract proves that these studies were commenced, and the memoir in question completed, before (and not, as stated by Professor M'Intosh,[1] after) the author's appointment to the Conservatorship of the Museum of the College of Surgeons, which did not take place till the year 1861. The brain of another monkey was also described in a paper on the anatomy of a South American species then known as *Pithecia monachus*, which appeared in the Zoological Society's *Proceedings* for 1862. In the following year (1863) he published, in the *Natural History Review*, a still more important communication, dealing with the brain of the Malay siamang (*Hylobates syndactylus*), one of the man-like apes, in which it was shown that in this species (and probably therefore in gibbons generally) the posterior part of the cerebrum, or main division of the brain, overlapped the cerebellum, or hind brain, to an even less degree than in the American howling-monkeys, which had hitherto been regarded as the lowest members of the group, so far as the feature in question was concerned. That such a feature should occur in one of the highest groups of apes was certainly a remarkable and unexpected discovery. Yet another contribution to the same subject was made in 1864, when a paper appeared in the Zoological Society's *Proceedings* on the brain of the red howling-monkey, then known as *Mycetes seniculus*, but of which the generic title is changed by many modern naturalists to *Alouata*.

The earlier memoirs of this series published (in the *Philosophical Transactions*), writes Professor M'Intosh in the *Scottish Review* for 1900, "formed important evidence

---

[1] *Scottish Review*, April, 1900, p. 5.

in the discussions which took place between Owen and Huxley in regard to the posterior lobe of the brain, the posterior cornu, and the hippocampus minor. Professor Owen, at the Cambridge Meeting of the British Association in 1862, maintained, from specimens of the human brain in spirit, and from a cast of the interior of the gorilla's skull, that in man the posterior lobes of the brain overlapped the cerebellum, whereas in the gorilla they did not ; that these characters are constant, and therefore he had decided to place man, with his overlapping posterior lobes, the existence of a posterior horn in the lateral ventricle, and the presence of a hippocampus minor in the posterior horn, under the special division Archencephala. Moreover, he grouped with these features the distinctive characters of the foot of man, and showed how it differed from that of all monkeys. Flower's accurate investigations enabled Huxley to substantiate his antagonistic position to Owen's doctrines, viz., that these structures, instead of being the attributes of man, are precisely the most marked cerebral characters common to man with the apes. Huxley also asserted that the differences between the foot of man and that of the higher apes were of the same order, and but slightly different in degree from those which separated one ape from another.

The result of this controversy was the overthrow (except in the mind and works of its author) of Owen's separation of man on the one hand as the representative of a primary group—the Archencephala ; and of apes, monkeys, Carnivora, Ungulates, Sirenians, and Cetaceans on the other hand, as forming a second group—the Gyrencephala.[1] As will be seen from the above quotation, this result was very largely due to the work of Flower, although it was brought into prominent notice by the superior fighting powers of Huxley, who was also an older, and at the time at anyrate, a better-known man. It may be added that Flower himself subsequently abandoned the use of the term " Quadru-mana," as distinguishing apes and monkeys on the one hand from man, as " Bimana," on the other, and brigaded all altogether under their Linnæan title " Pri-mates."

The contributions of Flower to our knowledge of (and, it may be added, to the clearing up of misconceptions in regard to) the mammalian brain, was, however, by no means confined to the Primates (man, apes, monkeys, and lemurs). On the contrary, his researches were of equal—if not indeed of more—importance with regard to the structure of that organ in the lower groups of the class, namely the marsupials and the monotremes (duckbill platypus and spiny ant-eater).

In the well-known Reade Lecture of 1859, Professor Owen expressed himself as follows with regard to the brain of the two groups last mentioned :—

" Prior to the year 1836, it was held by comparative anatomists that the brain in mammalia differed from that in all other vertebrate animals by the presence of the

---

[1] From the extract from Professor M'Intosh's notice of Flower's work above cited, it might be inferred that Owen first proposed the terms Archencephala, Gyrencephala, etc., at the Cambridge Meeting of the British Association in 1862. This is not so, as these terms were used by him in a paper read before the Linnæan Society in 1857, and also in his Reade Lecture " On the Classification and Geographical Distribution of the Mammalia," delivered at Cambridge on 10th May, 1859, and pub-lished in London (by J. W. Parker) as a separate volume the same year.

large mass of transverse white fibres called 'corpus callosum' by the anthropotomist; which fibres, over-arching the ventricles and diverging as they penetrate the substance of either hemisphere of the cerebrum, bring every convolution of the one into communication with those of the other hemisphere, whence the other name of this part—the 'great commissure.' In that year I discovered that the brain of the kangaroo, the wombat, and some other marsupial quadrupeds, wanted the 'great commissure'; and that the cerebral hemi-spheres were connected together, as in birds, only by the 'fornix' and 'anterior commissure.' Soon afterward I had the opportunity of determining that the same deficiency of structure prevailed in the *Ornithorhynchus* (duckbill) and *Echidna* (spiny ant-eater)."

Owen's conclusions with regard to the absence of the great connecting band of fibres between the hemispheres of the marsupial brain were first published in the *Philosophical Transactions* for 1837; those, with regard to the same lack in the monotremes, being added in Todd's *Cyclopædia of Anatomy and Physiology*, Article "Monotremata." In the latter article it was also stated that the brain of the echidna was further distinguished from that of other mammals by the circumstance that whereas in the latter the portion of the brain known as the optic lobes consists of four lobes (*corpora quadrigemina*), in the echidna and duckbill there are only a pair of such lobes (*corpora bigemina*.)

In consequence of this supposed lack of the corpus callosum in their brains, Owen separated the marsupials and monotremes from other mammals in a primary group by themselves, under the title of Lyencephala.

Flower's attack on these conclusions was commenced by a paper which appeared in the Zoological Society's *Proceedings* for 26th January 1864, entitled "On the Optic Lobes of the Brain of the Echidna," in which it was conclusively demonstrated that these structures resembled those of the higher mammals in being four-lobed.

More important still was his memoir "On the Commissures of the Cerebral Hemispheres of the Marsupialia and Monotremata, as compared with those of the Placental Mammals," which was published in the *Philosophical Transactions* of the Royal Society for 1865. In this was shown, it was thought, the existence in both monotremes and marsupials of a distinct, although very small, corpus callosum connecting the two hemispheres of the brain; the anterior commissure, which in the higher mammals is the smaller connecting band, being in this instance much the larger.

Recent researches have, however, tended to show that Owen was after all right in denying the existence of a corpus callosum in the latter groups. Even allowing for this correction, the result of this important paper was to discredit among all zoologists capable of forming an adequate opinion on the subject Owen's proposed fourfold division of the Mammalia into Lyencephala, Lissencephala, Gyrencephala, and Archencephala. And these terms have now completely disappeared from zoological literature.

In those days it required no considerable amount of courage to attack a man of Owen's established social and scientific position on an important subject like this; and Flower's triumph was therefore the more conspicuous. Of course such of these discoveries as are valid, if they had not been made by him, would have been made later on by somebody else, as they merely required accurate dissection and observation. But this may be said of every discovery of a like nature; and Flower is entitled to all credit for having worked out the subject in the way he did. It may be added, that, with our present knowledge of mammalian morphology, a classification based on the characters of the brain is manifestly based on a misconception from first to last; the degree of development and specialisation of that organ being purely adaptive features, and therefore not dependent upon structural relationships. Had Owen's classification been maintained, it would have been necessary to assign the primitive Carnivora and Ungulata to a group quite apart from the one containing their existing representatives.

In the light of modern research, it cannot now be held that the result of Flower's investigations in this direction was to demonstrate the existence of a corpus callosum to the brain in all the members of the mammalian class.

In another paper, dealing with the brain of the Javan loris, published in the *Transactions* of the Zoological Society, Flower made a further contribution to the study of this part of the organism. Previous to the appearance of the memoir on the marsupial and monotreme brain, Flower had published, in the *Natural History Review* for 1864, one on the number of cervical vertebræ in the Sirenia (manati and dugong). Apart from several papers on whales and dolphins, which, as already mentioned, are reserved for consideration in a later chapter, the next noteworthy zoological contribution from Flower's pen appears to be one on the gular pouch of the great bustard, published in the Zoological Society's *Proceedings* for 1865. This pouch, which, it may be observed is confined to the cock-bird, and inflated during the breeding season, is a very remarkable structure, which has recently been described in greater detail by Mr. W. P. Pycraft.

Two years later (1867), Flower contributed to the same journal a paper on the anatomy of the West African chevrotain, *Hyomoschus aquaticus,* or, as it is now called, *Dorcatherium aquaticum.* The specimen on which the paper was based was the first of its kind which had ever been dissected—at least in this country ; and the result of its examination was to confirm the view that the mouse-deer, or chevrotains, cannot be included among the true ruminants, or Pecora, but rather that they form a group (Tragulina), in many respects intermediate between the latter and the pigs and hippopotamuses, or Suina. To the essential difference between the chevrotains and the musk-deer, which have often been confounded, Flower was very fond of recurring in his later writings.

About the year 1866 Sir William began to turn his attention to the teeth of mammals, more especially as regards the mode in which the milk or baby series is succeeded by the permanent teeth, and the general homology of the milk with the permanent, and of the individual teeth of both series with one another. As the result of these investigations he published during the next few years the following papers on this subject. First and most important, one on the development and succession

of the teeth of marsupials, which appeared in the
Philosophical Transactions for 1867. In the following year
he delivered before the British Association at Norwich
a paper entitled " Remarks on the Homologies and Relation of the Teeth of the Mammalia," which was published
in the *Journal of Anatomy and Physiology* for the same
year. In that year he also published, in the *Proceedings*
of the Zoological Society, an account of the homology
and succession of the teeth in the armadillos. A general
sketch from his pen of the dentition of mammals
was published in the *British Medical Journal* for 1871,
while in the *Transactions* of the Odontological Society
for the same year, appeared a paper on the first, or milk,
dentition of the Mammalia.

By far the most important of this series of papers is
undoubtedly the one on the succession and homologies
of the teeth in the marsupials or pouched mammals ;
and it is the one which contains, perhaps, the most noteworthy discovery made by Flower.

Owen had previously pointed out that marsupials
differ from ordinary placental mammals in having four
(in place of three) pairs of cheek-teeth at the hinder
part of the series which have no milk, or deciduous,
predecessors, and are therefore, according to the usual
rule, to be regarded as true molars, in contradiction to
premolars, in which such deciduous predecessors are
generally developed. He considered, however, that all
the premolars in the kangaroo (and therefore presumably
in other marsupials) as well as the incisors or cutting
teeth, and the canines or tusks, were preceded by milk-
teeth. Flower, on the other hand (who it is only just
to add had a much fuller series of specimens of young

marsupials on which to work than was available to Owen), was enabled to show that in the Marsupialia only one pair of teeth in each jaw, at most, is preceded by a milk-tooth. The tooth, in question, is the fifth from the posterior end of the series, and whereas in the adult animal it differs in character from those behind it, its deciduous predecessor resembles the latter. The replacing tooth was further considered to correspond with the fourth or last premolar of placental mammals, while the replaced tooth was regarded as the only one in the entire series corresponding to the milk-teeth of placental mammals. This view rendered it necessary, of course, to regard all the four pairs of cheek-teeth behind this abnormal one as corresponding to the true molars of placentals, as had been done by Owen, thus making, as already mentioned, marsupials to differ from ordinary placentals by possessing four instead of three pairs of these teeth.

Before proceeding to notice an amendment which has been proposed in regard to the homology of the one successional tooth of the marsupials, certain other features connected with it and its predecessor discussed by Flower may be briefly mentioned. He noticed, to quote from an admirable epitome of his observations on this point, drawn up by Professor M'Intosh in the *Scottish Review* for 1900, " that there were considerable differences in the various genera as to the relative period of the animal's life at which the fall of the temporary molar and the evolution of its successor takes place. In some, as in the rat-kangaroos, it is one of the latest, the temporary tooth retaining its place and its functions until the animal has nearly, if not quite, reached its full growth, and is not shed until all the other teeth are in position and use.   On the other hand, in the Tasmanian wolf the temporary tooth is very rudimentary in size and form, and is shed or absorbed before any other teeth enter the gum.   Anterior to the period of Sir William Flower's communication, mammals had been, in regard to the succession of their teeth, divided into two groups—the Monophyodonts, or those that generate a single series of teeth, and the Diphyodonts, or those that develop two sets of teeth, but, as he pointed out, even in the most typical Diphyodonts the successional process does not extend to the whole of the teeth, always stopping short of those situated most posteriorly in each series.   The pouched animals (marsupials), he stated, occupied an intermediate position, presenting, as it were, a rudimentary diphyodont condition, the successional process being confined to a single tooth on each side of each jaw."

All this is unexceptionable.   Flower, however, went further than this, and claimed that the true molar teeth of mammals correspond serially with the permanent premolars, canines, and incisors, and not with their deciduous predecessors.   And he therefore urged (as indeed must be the case on these premisses) that the whole dentition of adult marsupials corresponds with the permanent dentition of placentals.   A further inference from this is that the milk-teeth, instead of being an original development, may rather be a set superadded to meet the temporary needs of mammals whose permanent set is of a highly complex type.

To review the objections which have been raised against these views would be entering on a very difficult question, and one in regard to which uniformity of opinion by no means exists among naturalists even at the present day. It may be mentioned, however, that from the circumstance of the later milk-premolars resembling (as was noticed by Flower in the case of the one tooth replaced in marsupials) the true molars rather than the permanent premolars, it has been suggested that the milk-dentition is serially homologous with the true molars. And on this view, the entire dentition of marsupials (with the exception of the one replacing tooth) corresponds to the milk-dentition of placentals. Possibly, however, the larger number of incisors which distinguish many of the carnivorous marsupials from the placentals may be due to the development of teeth belonging to the permanent series with those of the milk-set, and both persisting together throughout life. Be this as it may, it is evident, on the above view of the serial homology of their dentition, that marsupials, instead of as Flower supposed, showing the commencement of a milk-dentition, really exhibit the decadence of the permanent series.

In this respect they display a precise similarity to the modern elephants, as indeed was pointed out by Flower in his original paper, although on a false premiss, for he at that time regarded the anterior cheek-teeth of the elephant as the representatives of the permanent premolars, whereas they really correspond with the milk-premolars.

One objection has indeed been raised with regard to the identification of the adult marsupial dentition with the milk-set of placentals, namely, the existence in certain marsupialia of rudimentary teeth belonging to an earlier

H

set than the one functionally developed. This has been got over by regarding these rudimentary germs as the representatives of a prelacteal series.

Passing on to another point, it has to be noticed that exception has also been taken to Flower's view that the replacing tooth of marsupials and its deciduous predecessor correspond to the fourth, or last premolar of placentals. The question has been discussed in considerable detail in the Zoological Society's *Proceedings* for 1899 by the present writer, who had for material the dentition of certain extinct South American mammals quite unknown to science at the time Flower's paper was written. The result of these comparisons was to render it evident, in the present writer's opinion, that the replacing tooth of the marsupials corresponds to the third, instead of to the fourth, premolar of placentals. From this it follows that marsupials agree with placentals in possessing only three pairs of true molars; the first of the four teeth in the former behind the replacing tooth being the last milk-premolar (which is never replaced) instead of, as supposed by Flower, the first true molar. This conclusion, as pointed out by the present writer in the paper referred to above, had really been arrived at years previously by Owen, who also believed the replacing tooth to correspond to the third premolar of placentals.

In thus bringing marsupials into line with placentals as regards their dentition, this later interpretation accords well with recent discoveries in regard to other parts of the organisation of the former animals. It should, however, be mentioned that the newer view is by no means accepted by all zoologists, although it has received the support of the well-known American paleontologist, Dr. J. L. Wortman,[1] who is specially qualified to form a trustworthy opinion on a point of this nature.

Finally, whatever be the eventual verdict as to the serial homology of the marsupial dentition as a whole, and also as to that of the replacing premolar, Flower must always be credited with the discovery that marsupials replace only a single pair of teeth in each jaw by vertical successors.

The other papers on dentition referred to above as having been written by Flower about the same time are, although interesting in their way, of far less importance than the one published in the *Philosophical Transactions*. Indeed the one read before the British Association in 1868 and published in the *Journal of Anatomy and Physiology* for the same year, is little more than a recapitulation of the results arrived at in the former.

The paper on the development and succession of the teeth in the armadillos, published in the Zoological Society's *Proceedings* in 1868, is, on the other hand, of considerable interest on account of its confirming the fact first mentioned by the French zoologist, Professor Paul Gervais, but generally overlooked by subsequent writers up to that time, that the common nine-banded armadillo (*Tatusia peba*) differs from its relatives in replacing some of its teeth by vertical successors. This at the time was an unexpected feature in any member of the so-called Edentate mammals; and tended further to break down the supposed hard and fast distinction between monophyodonts and diphyodonts.

[1] *American Journal of Science*, vol. xi. p. 336 (1901).

Closely connected with the subject of dentition is a paper on " The Affinities and Probable Habits of the Extinct Marsupial, *Thylacoleo carnifex* (Owen)," communicated by Flower to the Geological Society of London in 1868, and published in the *Quarterly Journal* of that body for the same year. After alluding to the paper on marsupial dentition, Professor Ray Lankester, in his obituary notice of Sir William in *Nature*, of 13th July 1899, observes of the communication under consideration that—" The next most striking discovery which we owe to Flower seems to me to be the complete and convincing demonstration that the extinct marsupial, called *Thylacoleo carnifex* by Owen, was not a carnivore, but a gnawing herbivorous creature like the marsupial rats and the wombat—a demonstration which has been brought home to the eye even of the unlearned by the complete restoration of the skull of *Thylacoleo* in the Natural History Museum by Dr. Henry Woodward."

If we are to believe later authorities, Flower's demonstration of the herbivorous nature of the creature in question was by no means so " complete and convincing " as the learned Professor would have us believe ; but of this anon.

The first important paper on *Thylacoleo*, which was a creature of the approximate size of a jaguar, whose remains are met with in the superficial formations of Australia, was one by Owen, published in the *Philosophical Transactions* for 1859. From the general characters of the skull (which was at that time only known by fragments), and especially from the rudimentary condition of the hinder cheek-teeth and the enormous size of the secant replacing premolar, which

bears a certain superficial resemblance to the carnassial
tooth of the cats, its describer was led to the conclusion
that *Thylacoleo* was a marsupial carnivore, and "one of
the fellest and most destructive of predatory beasts."
Probably Owen's views at this time were, that the
creature had its nearest living relatives in the members
of the Australian family *Dasyuridæ*, such as the
Tasmanian devil (*Sarcophilus ursinus*), and that it bore a
relationship to the existing carnivorous marsupials somewhat similar to that presented by a lion to a dog. At
this time there was no evidence to show whether the
large teeth near the front of the jaw, the existence of
which was indicated in the original specimen merely by
its empty socket, was a canine or an incisor; and though
Owen was inclined to regard it as the former, he admitted that it might be an incisor, in which event he
recognised that the affinities of the animal would be
more with the herbivorous, or diprotodont section of
the marsupials, and more especially the phalangers, or so-
called opossums of the colonists. This is clearly indicated by the following sentence appended by Sir
Richard to his discription :—"If, however, this be
really the foremost tooth of the jaw, it would be one of
a pair of terminal incisors according to the marsupial
type exhibited by the *Macropodidæ* (kangaroos) and
Phalangistidæ (phalangers)."

In 1866, after receiving additional specimens from
Australia, Owen was enabled to describe the greater
part of the skull and the entire dentition of *Thylacoleo*.
The large anterior teeth were clearly recognised to be
incisors, which, in Owen's opinion, "proved the
Thylacoleo to be the carnivorous modification of the

more common and characteristic type of Australian marsupials, having the incisors of the lower jaw reduced to a pair of large, more or less procumbent and approximately conical teeth, or 'tusks.'" Not only did the additional evidence serve to confirm Sir Richard in his view of the carnivorous propensities of *Thylacoleo*, but he considered that in this extinct form we have "the simplest and most effectual dental machinery for predatory life and carnivorous diet known in the mammalian class. It is the extreme modification, to this end, of the diprotodont type of marsupialia."

Beyond, however, admitting its affinities with the diprotodonts, Sir Richard Owen does not appear in this later paper to have regarded *Thylacoleo* as a near relative of any of the existing forms; but in the article on "Paleontology" in the eighth edition of the *Encyclopædia Britannica*, published in 1859, he seems to have considered it allied to *Plagiaulax* of the Purbeck strata of Dorsetshire, which had been shown by Dr. Hugh Falconer to be probably of herbivorous habits.

Sir William Flower, in the aforesaid paper in the Geological Society's *Quarterly Journal* for 1868, while agreeing with Owen that *Thylacoleo* was related to the diprotodont rather than to the polyprotodont carnivorous marsupials, differed from the conclusion that it was a carnivore. While the large cutting premolar teeth were considered by Owen to resemble the carnassial teeth of a lion, Flower was struck by their similarity to the corresponding teeth of the rat-kangaroos and the phalangers. After discussing the other teeth, he concluded that "in the number and arrangement of these teeth . . . *Thylacoleo* corresponds exactly with the modern families *Macropodidæ* and *Phalangistidæ*, and differs completely from the carnivorous marsupials."

After alluding to the small size of the brain-cavity and the large space for the attachment of the powerful muscles which worked the lower jaw, and suggesting that these features may be only to be expected in a large form as compared with the smaller members of the same group, Flower concluded that the habits of all species with the same general type of dentition must necessarily be similar.   And, on these premisses, it was urged that *Thylacoleo* must in all probability have been a vegetable-feeder.   The large premolar may seemingly have been "as well adapted for chopping up succulent roots and vegetables, as for dividing the nutritive fibres of animal prey."   It is further suggested that the nutriment of *Thylacoleo* "may have been some kind of root or bulb; it may have been fruit; it may have been flesh."   While in conclusion it is argued that the organisation of the animal did not countenance the idea of its preying on the large contemporary marsupials.

Omitting reference to Owen's reply to this reversal of his conclusions, and also to certain comments and additions to the arguments by other writers, we may pass on to a paper by Dr. R. Broom, published in the *Proceedings* of the Linnean Society of New South Wales for April 1898, and entitled "On the Affinities and Habits of *Thylacoleo*."

In this the author admits that the animal in question, as suggested by Owen in his second paper, and more fully determined by Flower, was undoubtedly a diprotodont, and that it was nearly allied to the modern phalangers.   With the latter it is indeed closely connected by the recently discovered extinct *Burramys*, which differs from the existing members of that group by the large size of the secant premolar.

After discussing numerous points in connection with the problem, Dr. Broom states that those who believe *Thylacoleo* to have been carnivorous, " evidently consider that the molars have been reduced through their functions being taken up by the large premolars. But could the large premolars take up the molar function—could they grind? Even those who favour the idea of *Thylacoleo* being a vegetable-feeder, admit that the premolars were cutting teeth, and the difficulty of imagining a herbivorous animal without grinders is got over by supposing that its food was of a soft or succulent nature."

But for the creature to have lived on succulent roots and bulbs, the vegetation of that part of Australia where it lived must, urges Dr. Broom, have been quite different from what it is at the present day; and we have no justification for assuming any such change to have taken place. Moreover, an animal that could only slice, and not grind up, vegetable food, could apparently subsist only on ripe fruit, and such is to be met with in Australia only at one season of the year, when, owing to the abundance of frugivorous mammals, little, if any, is allowed to fall to the ground.

"It is probably however," adds Dr. Broom, "unnecessary to discuss further what food *Thylacoleo* could possibly have obtained, when we have, as I hold with Owen, the most satisfactory proof from its anatomical structure as to what food it did obtain. It must be admitted that *Thylacoleo* had enormous temporal muscles, and it is perfectly certain that such muscles would not

have been developed unless the animal required them.
For what could such powerful muscles be required?
Most certainly not for slicing fruits or succulent roots
and bulbs, nor would they be required even for the
slicing of fleshy fibres. Temporal muscles are chiefly
used apparently for closing the jaws more or less forcibly
from the open position, while for the more complicated
movements of mastication it is the masseter and pterygoid
muscles that are chiefly used. Hence in all carnivorous
animals the temporals are largely developed and the
masseters more feebly, because the killing process
requires a very forcible closing of the jaws, and the
work to be done by the premolars and molars is comparatively little. In herbivorous animals the conditions
are reversed. The jaws are here rarely required to be
opened widely or to be closed with any great force,
while a very large amount of grinding work has to be
done; hence the temporals are rarely much larger than
the masseters, and often very much smaller. When
we look at *Thylacoleo*, we find not only the enormous
temporals and only moderate masseters, but everything
else about the skull seems to be built on carnivorous
lines. Owen has shown the wonderful similarity which
exists between the molar machinery in *Thylacoleo* and
the lion, and it is hard to conceive as possible any other
cause giving rise to such a specialisation in *Thylacoleo*
than that which led to a similar specialisation in the cat
tribe. Another most striking feature is to be seen in
the condition of the incisors. Leaving out of consideration the mode of implantation and structure of the teeth
—both confirmatory of the carnivorous hypothesis—
there is one point which appears to me absolutely con-

clusive on the subject. Unless Owen's figures are altogether unreliable, the lower incisors are quite unlike those of the herbivorous diprotodonts. In such typical forms as the wombat, the koala, the kangaroo, and the phalanger, though there are different modifications of the arrangement, we have the lower incisors meeting the upper, and forming with them an instrument for biting through a moderately tough, fibrous tissue, and even in the very small diprotodonts, so far as I am aware, the lower incisors always meet and work against the upper. But in *Thylacoleo* we have powerful pointed incisors which do not meet, but overlap. Though technically incisors, they are not intended to incise, but to pierce and tear. Such powerful pointed and over-lapping teeth, though easily explained on the theory that they were intended to kill and tear animal prey, were never surely provided merely to pierce succulent vegetables or ripe fruit. It might of course be argued that the incisors were used as weapons of defence, as apparently are the canines in the baboon; but against this idea is the objection that the incisors were put to some use which wore them down and blunted them more rapidly than would be the case if they were chiefly used on the rare occasions when the animal had to defend itself; and furthermore, were such the case, the temporals would not require to be greatly developed.

"There is thus, in my opinion, no other conclusion tenable than that *Thylacoleo* was a purely carnivorous animal, and one which would be quite able to, and pro-bably did, kill animals as large as or larger than itself."

This opinion as to the carnivorous habits of *Thylacoleo* is approved by Mr. B. A. Bensley, who has specially studied the Australian marsupials in a memoir recently published in the *Transactions* of the Linnean Society of London.

If it be correct, it reduces the net result of Flower's investigations on this subject to a fuller realisation of the diprotodont affinities of the animal under consideration.

In the latter part of 1868, Mr. Flower, as he was then styled, communicated to the Zoological Society a most important paper entitled, "On the Value of the Characters of the Base of the Cranium in the Classification of the Order Carnivora," which was published in the first part of the Society's *Proceedings* for the following year. Working on the lines suggested twenty years previously by Mr. H. N. Turner, who had pointed out the importance of certain peculiarities of the base of the skull in the Mammalia, and especially demonstrated their constancy in the different groups of the Carnivora, Flower felt himself justified in dividing, on these characters, the existing terrestrial representatives of that order into three groups. These were—1st, the Æluroidea, comprising the cats (*Felidæ*), the fossa (*Cryptoproctidæ*), civets and mongooses (*Viverridæ*), the aard-wolf (*Proteleidæ*), and hyænas (*Hyænidæ*); 2nd, the Cynoidea, including only the dogs, wolves, and foxes; and 3rd, the Arctoidea, embracing the bears (*Ursidæ*), the raccoons and pandas (*Procyonidæ* and *Æluridæ*), and the weasels, badgers, otters, etc. (*Mustelidæ*).

One result of this classification from cranial characteristics was to determine definitely the position of the American cacomistle (*Bassaris* or *Bassariscus*), which had been previously uncertain. The genus, as might have been expected from distributional considerations, turned out to belong to the raccoon family (*Procyonidæ*).

As regards the relationship of the three main groups, subsequent palæontological discoveries have fully confirmed Flower's view that the *Canidæ* (Cynoidea) occupy a central, or perhaps rather a basal, position. Palæontology has, however, also shown that the bears (*Ursidæ*) are a direct offshoot from the *Canidæ*, and accordingly that, if extinct forms be taken into consideration, there is no justification for the separation of the two families into distinct primary groups (Arctoidea and Cynoidea). On the other hand, fossil forms from the Lower Tertiaries of France and of North America seem to demonstrate the existence of a complete gradation between the primitive dogs (*Canidæ*) and the ancestral civets (*Viverridæ*), thus breaking up the distinction between the Cynoidea and the Æluroidea. Nor is this all, for according to the French palæontologists, there exists a transition between the primitive civets and the early weasels (*Mustelidæ*); which, with what has been already stated in connection with the bears, indicates that the Arctoidea is a more or less artificial group, the members of which have come to resemble one another to a certain degree in regard to the characters of the base of the skull, owing to "parallelism." In this connection it is somewhat curious to note that a certain resemblance, which had been pointed out by Turner as existing between the mongooses or ichneumons (*Viverridæ*) and the weasels, was regarded by Flower as of no importance. Finally, it is by no means improbable that the cats (*Felidæ*) have no near kinship with the civets, but may be directly sprung from more primitive Carnivora.

It is thus evident that Flower's proposed triple division of the Carnivora is not altogether in accord with palæontological, or phylogenetic, evidence. An amendment is to merge the Cynoidea in the Arctoidea, and thus retain only two groups. The observations recorded in the paper have a high permanent value, in respect to the structure of the carnivorous skull.

Another paper by Flower appeared in the Zoological Society's *Proceedings* for 1869, dealing with the anatomy of the soft parts of that remarkable animal, the African aard-wolf (*Proteles cristatus*). Although the skeleton had been previously described, no information had hitherto been available with regard to the viscera. In the paper discussed in the foregoing paragraphs Flower, from the external characters, coupled with those of the dentition and skeleton, had regarded the creature as the representative of a distinct family, intermediate in some respects between the *Hyænidæ* and the *Viverridæ*. The result of the examination of the viscera was in the main to support this conclusion, although it showed that the *Proteleidæ* are more closely allied to the *Hyænidæ* than the author had previously believed to be the case. The aard-wolf may, indeed, be regarded as a kind of small and degraded hyæna, with an almost rudimentary type of dentition, suitable to the soft substances on which it feeds.

Passing on to the year 1870, we have to note the appearance of two separate works bearing Flower's name. The first of these was the *Introductory Lectures to the Course of Comparative Anatomy*, delivered at the Royal College of Surgeons in that year.

Far more important was the issue of the first edition of that invaluable text-book, *An Introduction to the Osteology of the Mammalia.* Since, however, mention of this work had been already made in an earlier chapter, it need not be further alluded to in this place.

During the same year, exclusive of those on the Cetacea, several papers were published by Flower in various scientific serials. Among these, bare mention must suffice for one, "On the Connexion of the Hyoid Arch with the Cranium," which appeared in the twentieth volume of the *Report* of the British Association. More important is the article "On the Correspondence between the parts composing the Shoulder and the Pelvic Girdle of the Mammalia." In this the author pointed out that although the homology between the scapula in the shoulder-girdle and the ilium in the pelvis had long been admitted by naturalists, yet much misconception existed with regard to the exact correspondence between the respective surfaces and borders of these bones; and he then proceeded to define and describe these correspondences in considerable detail. The names then assigned by Flower to the component surfaces and borders of the bones in question have ever since been generally adapted by naturalists. Observations were also recorded with regard to the homology between the coracoid bone and the ischium. A second paper in the same journal for 1870 dealt with the carpus of the dog; while in 1873 he published in this medium a note on the same part of the skeleton in the sloths.

Reverting once more to the *Proceedings* of the Zoological Society, in which the bulk of his contributions to the anatomy of mammals was published, we find a paper by Flower in the volume for 1870 on the anatomy of the Himalayan panda (*Ælurus fulgens.*)

The specimen on which the paper was based was the first example of this remarkable animal which had ever been dissected; and the brain and viscera were described at considerable length. The result of the dissection was to confirm the author's previous opinion—based on the external characters and skeleton—as to the near affinity of *Ælurus* to the American *Procyonidæ*; and it was left somewhat an open question, whether it should be included in that group, or regarded as the representative of a family (*Æluridæ*) by itself. In after years Mr. W. T. Blanford adopted the former view. In the following year (1871) Flower contributed a note to the *Proceedings*, recording the occurrence of a specimen of the ringed seal (*Phoca hispida*) on the Norfolk coast in 1846; and he also wrote a paper in the same volume on the skeleton of one of the cassowaries. The somewhat remarkable fact that the two-spotted palm-civet (*Nandinia binotata*) differs from the other genera of the same group by the absence of a blind appendage, or cæcum, to the intestine, was recorded by Flower in the same serial for 1872.

Of much more importance than either of the foregoing were two contributions to mammalian anatomy made by Sir William during the year last mentioned. The one, which appeared in the *Medical Times and Gazette*, was the report of " Lectures on the Comparative Anatomy of the Organs of Digestion in the Mammalia, delivered at the Royal College of Surgeons in February and March, 1872.' In this article, which is well illustrated, will be found descriptions of the various forms assumed by the stomach in a large number of the ordinal and family groups; especial attention being directed to the remarkable complexity of that organ in the porpoise. The other, which was published in *Nature*, and in abstract in the *Report* of the British Association, dealt with the arrangement and nomenclature of the lobes of the mammalian liver. It is, perhaps, one of the most valuable of the author's contributions to visceral anatomy; and introduced order and precision where confusion had previously reigned. The names then given to the different lobes of the liver have been very generally adopted in zoological and anatomical literature.

In 1873 Flower delivered before the Royal Institution a lecture on palæontological evidence of gradual modification of animal forms, which is published in the *Proceedings* of that body for the same year. In this he touched on the important evidence afforded by the discoveries which had then been recently made in North America in favour of the derivation of one animal form from another, directing particular attention to the case for the evolution of the horse. Another paper on the same subject appears in the *British Medical Journal* for 1874; while, as noticed below, Sir William again lectured on palæontological evolution in 1876.

The year 1874 was noteworthy, so far as palæontology is concerned, by the appearance in the *Philosophical Transactions* of the Royal Society of a paper by Flower on part of a remarkable mammalian skull from Patagonia, described under the name of *Homalodontotherium cunninghami*. In justice to the author, it should be said that he was not responsible for the undue length of the generic name, which had been bestowed by his friend Huxley four years previously in the Geological Society's *Journal*, and which Flower was therefore compelled to employ. It refers to the fact that the jaws of the new animal are remarkable for the even and unbroken wall formed by the teeth, which show no enlarged tusks. At the time the geological age of this interesting fossil was quite unknown; but it formed the forerunner of the marvellous discoveries of the remains of fossil mammals of middle tertiary age in Patagonia, which have been made of late years, and have done so much to increase our knowledge of the past life and history of the South American Continent.

Of minor interest is a paper by the then Hunterian Professor in the *Quarterly Journal* of the Geological Society on a much rolled and battered skull from the so-called Red Crag of Suffolk, which the author referred to a species of that extinct genus of sea-cows (Sirenia) known as *Halitherium*. Such interest as the specimen possessed was due to its affording the first evidence of the occurrence of remains of that genus in Britain. Another paper, it may be mentioned, was published by Flower in the same journal for 1877, in which another well-known extinct continental genus of mammals was added to the fauna of the Red Crag of East Anglia. The paper described two molar teeth, in the York Museum, from the deposit in question, evidently referable to the large bear-like animal known as *Hyænarctus*, of which the first remains had been described many years previously from the Siwalik Hills of North-Eastern India. As the mention of this paper has broken the chronological order of treatment, it may be added that in 1876 Flower published another paper, this time in the Zoological Society's *Proceedings*, on a mammalian skull from the Red Crag. The specimen referred to in this communication was provisionally assigned to Cuvier's genus *Xiphodon*, and was believed to have been originally washed out from a formation much older than the Red Crag, and reburied in the latter.

Next on our list comes a paper on the anatomy of the musk-deer (*Moschus moschiferus*), contributed to the serial last cited for 1875, in which the author points out how widely this animal differs from the more typical deer, and shows that it cannot even claim a near relationship with the Chinese water-deer, despite the fact that in both species the males are devoid of antlers, and are armed with long sabre-like tusks in the upper jaw. In several respects—notably the presence of a gall-bladder to the liver—the musk-deer is indeed nearer to the hollow-horned ruminants (Bovidæ), than to the other members of the deer tribe (Cervidæ).

In 1876 Professor Flower delivered before the Royal Institution an extremely interesting lecture on the extinct mammals of North America, which at that time were in course of being made known to the scientific world by the writings of Professors Marsh and Cope. In the course of this lecture Flower alluded at considerable length to the ancestry of the horse—then a comparatively new subject—and also discussed the structure and affinities of those gigantic many-horned mammals commonly known as Dinocerata. In concluding, the lecturer observed that the work accomplished in America taught us—"First, that the living world around us at the present moment bears but an exceedingly small proportion to the whole series of animal and vegetable forms which have existed in past ages. Secondly, that, notwithstanding all that has been said, and most justly said, of the necessary imperfection of the geological record, we may hope that there is still so much preserved that the study of the course of events which have led up to the present condition of life on the globe, may have a great future before it."

The subsequent discoveries of fossil mammalian remains in such enormous quantities in Patagonia, and still later in the Libyan desert, have rendered this utterance almost prophetic.

During the same year (1876) appeared, in the *Philosophical Transactions*, a notice by Flower of the seals and cetaceans obtained during the *Transit of Venus* expeditions of 1874 and 1875. The year 1876 likewise witnessed the publication, in the *Proceedings* of the Zoological Society, of an article on the skulls of the various existing species of rhinoceroses, in which it was shown that the number of such species had been altogether unjustifiably exaggerated by the late Dr. J. E. Gray and other writers, and that in all probability there were really not more than five. Certain characters connected with the postero-lateral region of the skull were also described, which served to divide these species into groups. A further contribution to our knowledge of the skulls of the rhinoceroses was made by Flower in 1878, when he described, in the same journal, the skull of an Indian specimen, which it was thought might be the *Rhinoceros lasiotis* of Dr. Sclater—now known to be (as then suggested) merely a local race of the two-horned *R. sumatrensis*.

Between the years 1880 and 1883 several papers on mammalian zoology were published by Flower in the *Proceedings* of the Zoological Society and elsewhere, none of which can be regarded as of first-rate importance. The first of these (*P.Z.S.* 1880) dealt with the internal anatomy of that rare mammal, the bush-dog (*Speothus,* or *Icticyon, venaticus*), of Guiana, which had never previously been described. The author regarded this animal as a specialised member of the Canidæ, showing some signs of affinity with the wild dogs (*Cyon*) of Asia. In 1880 the museum of the Royal College of Surgeons received a very large skull of the elephant-seal or sea-elephant (*Macrorhinus leoninus*); and this induced Flower to draw up some notes on that enormous creature, which appeared in the above-named journal for 1881. The author described it as "an animal which, notwithstanding its former abundance and wide distribution, and its great zoological interest, is still very imperfectly known anatomically, and very poorly represented in collections." Fortunately, since that date—mainly owing to the energy and liberality of Mr. Rothschild—specimens of the skin and skeleton of this huge seal have been secured for our museums before it was too late. In the same volume Flower drew attention to the evidence showing that the sea-cow, or manati, of which a pair were living at the time in the Brighton Aquarium, occasionally, or periodically, comes ashore for the purpose of grazing. In the same year appeared an article from his pen in the *British Medical Journal* on the anatomy of the Cetacea and Edentata; while in 1882 the question of the mutual relationships of the mammals commonly included in the latter order (such as sloths, ant-eaters, armadillos, pangolins, and aard-varks) were discussed by him in the *Proceedings* of the Zoological Society.

The trend of the paper last mentioned, as well as that of some of his other communications published shortly before, indicates that about this time, instead of restricting his attention more or less entirely to their anatomy, Flower was much occupied with the subject of the classification of the Mammalia. And the reason is not far to seek, for he had undertaken not only the volume of the "Catalogue of Osteological Specimens in the Museum of the Royal College of Surgeons," dealing with mammals other than man, but he had likewise engaged (in co-operation with the late Dr. Dobson) to write the article "Mammalia" for the ninth edition of the *Encyclopædia Britannica.* With the view apparently of clearing the way for these two important contributions to zoology, he published during the early part of 1883 in the Zoological Society's *Proceedings* a paper on the " Arrangement of the Orders and Families of Mammalia."

To discuss this important paper in detail on the present occasion is quite unnecessary; and it will suffice to state that it has formed the basis on which all modern classifications of the group are framed. Indeed it has been accepted by most writers with little or no modification. In this scheme it was proposed to divide mammals into three primary groups, or sub-classes, namely, Prototheria, or Ornithodelphia, as represented only by the egg-laying group; Metatheria or Didelphia, including the pouched group, or marsupials; and Eutheria or Monodelphia, comprising the whole of the remaining or placental groups. Of late years, owing to the discovery of unexpected relationships between placentals and marsupials, it has been proposed to recognise only two sub-classes of mammals: the Eutheria, comprising the two groups last mentioned, and the Prototheria, or monotremes. The scheme chiefly differed from the one proposed some years earlier by Huxley in the inclusion of the Hyracoidea (klipdass) and Proboscidea (elephants) as sub-orders of the Ungulata, instead of their forming separate orders by themselves.   In this instance Flower ranked the Artiodactyla, Perissodactyla, Hyracoidea, and Proboscidea as equivalent sub-orders of Ungulata, but later on he brigaded the two former together as Ungulata Vera, and the two latter as Subungulata.

The above scheme was employed by Flower in the article " Mammalia," written by him for the ninth edition of the *Encyclopædia Britannica*, the volume containing which appeared in 1883. This article, with others by himself and other authors, formed, as will be noticed later on, the basis of the *Study of Mammals* published in 1891. Among other articles contributed by Flower to the *Encyclopædia* were those on the Horse, Kangaroo, Lemur, Lion, Mastodon, Megatherium, Otter, Platypus, Rhinoceros, Seal, Swine, Tapir, Whale, and Zebra.

The aforesaid scheme of classification was likewise used in the second part of the " Catalogue of Osteological Specimens in the Museum of the Royal College of Surgeons," which was written with the assistance of Dr. Garson, and appeared in 1884. Since this valuable work has been already noticed at some length in the chapter devoted to Flower's official connection with the

College of Surgeons, it need not be further referred to in this place, except that the writer may again take the opportunity of expressing his regret that the views on nomenclature there enunciated have not met with acceptance among the modern school of naturalists.

At the "Jubilee" meeting of the Zoological Society, held in June 1887, Flower, as President, read an address on the "Progress of Zoological Science" during the reign of Queen Victoria, which appeared in the *Report* of the Council of that year, and to which reference has been made in an earlier chapter.

About this time the Natural History Museum received a series of antlers shed year by year by one particular red-deer stag, together with the complete skull and antlers of the same animal; and this gift induced Flower to deliver in December 1887 a lecture on "Horns and Antlers" before the Middlesex Natural History Society, which is printed, with a plate of the aforesaid series of red-deer antlers, in a somewhat abbreviated form, in the *Transactions* of that Society.

If we except a few on Cetacea, noticed in the next chapter, Sir William's contributions to the Zoological Society's *Proceedings* after 1883 were not numerous or of much importance. In 1884 he contributed, however, remarks on the so-called white elephant from Burma, then exhibited in the Society's Menagerie; and in the same year he also wrote on the young dentition of the capibara. In 1887 he discussed the generic position and relationships of the pigmy hippopotamus of Liberia. The acquisition in the following year by the Natural History Museum of specimens of that breed of Japanese fowls remarkable for the excessive elongation of the tail-feathers of the cocks, led to a note on that subject in the *Proceedings* for the same year. This paper, it may be incidentally mentioned, is noteworthy, on account of the evidence it affords that Sir William did not regard the variations displayed by domesticated animals as in any way unworthy the notice of the naturalist; while the next shows that monstrosities or abnormalities —at all events to a certain extent—are also worthy of recognition. The note incidentally alluded to in the last sentence appeared in 1889, and dealt with an African rhinoceros head, showing three horns. Finally, in 1890, Sir William exhibited and commented upon a photograph of the nesting-hole of a hornbill, showing the female " walled up" with mud.

The next year (1891) saw the publication of *An Introduction to the Study of Mammals, Living and Extinct,* written, as already said, in collaboration with the present writer, and embodying the whole of Flower's contributions to the *Encyclopædia Britannica,* together with certain articles by other authors from the same work, and such new material as was necessary in order to weave these *disjecta membra* into one connected and harmonious whole.

In the same year was also published, in the *Modern Science Series,* Sir William's admirable little volume on *The Horse,* which was likewise largely based on his *Encyclopædia* articles. In this work Flower dwelt particularly on the vestiges exhibited by the modern horse of its descent from more generalised ancestors; and he was successful in demonstrating that the structure known to veterinarians as the " ergot," represents one of the foot-pads of the earlier forms.

Undoubtedly the most important elements in the foregoing tale of work are those relating to the mammalian (and especially the marsupial) brain, and the marsupial dentition. And if Flower had accomplished nothing more than this, he would have been entitled to gratitude of his successors. But, as we shall immediately see, all the above formed but a portion of his zoological labours.

CHAPTER VI

WORK ON THE CETACEA

NEXT at any rate to the study of the various races of the human species (which he took up seriously later on in his career), the group of mammals to which Flower devoted special attention, and which attracted his greatest interest, was undoubtedly that of the Cetacea, or whales, dolphins, porpoises, etc. At the time when he set himself seriously to study these aquatic and fish-like mammals, the zoology of the group was certainly in a most confused and unsatisfactory state; partly, no doubt, owing to the comparative rarity of complete specimens in our museums, and the consequent difficulty of instituting accurate comparisons, and partly to the reckless prodigality with which names had been given to imperfect or insufficiently characterised specimens by some of his predecessors and early contemporaries, and the needless multiplication of generic terms. It was consequently at this time almost impossible to be sure which was the right name for even many of the commoner species; while in the case of the rarer kinds, the confusion was almost hopeless. When Flower left the subject—which he only did when his working days were over—it was in great measure thoroughly in order, although of course much was left for future workers to fill in. Unhappily, his views on the nomenclature of the group have not been accepted by all his followers; so that a fresh and totally unnecessary source of confusion has been introduced of late years into a subject which had already sufficient difficulties of its own.

In regard to the discrimination of species, Flower took a view almost the reverse of that held by some of his predecessors and colleagues; and, as he says himself, he may have consequently erred in a direction the very opposite of theirs. " As species have not generally been recognised as such," he wrote in the British Museum *List* of 1885, " unless presenting constant distinguishing characters capable of definition, it is probable that, in the imperfect state of knowledge of many forms, some may have been grouped together which a fuller acquaintance with all parts of their structure, external and internal, will show to be distinct."

Apart from his explaining to popular audiences that whales were mammals and not fishes, Flower emphasised three points very strongly in regard to the organisation and physiology of these animals. First of all, he pointed out that, as a rule, they do not " spout " water from their " blowholes." " The ' spouting,' or more properly the ' blowing ' of the whale," he wrote, " is nothing more than the ordinary act of expiration, which, taking place at larger intervals than in land animals, is performed with a greater amount of emphasis. The moment the animal rises to the surface it forcibly expels from its lungs the air taken in at the last inspiration, which is of course highly charged with watery vapour in consequence of the natural respiratory changes. This, rapidly condensing in the cold atmosphere in which the phenomena is generally observed, forms a column of steam or spray, which has been erroneously taken for water."

Secondly, he drew attention to the importance of the rudiments of hind-limbs which occur in many whales as affording decisive evidence of the descent of the group from land mammals. And thirdly, he emphasised the marked distinction between baleen, or whalebone, whales (Mystacoceti), and toothed whales and dolphins (Odontoceti); although he appears never to have gone so far in this direction as some modern naturalists, who are of opinion that these two groups have originated independently of one another from separate types of land mammals.

Another point to which Flower devoted a considerable share of attention was the dimensions attained by the larger species of whales. Previously, there is no doubt that very great exaggeration had been current in this respect, and that such things as 150-feet whales are unknown. With his excessive caution, and determination to be on the safe side, it is however probable that in some instances—notably the Greenland right-whale and the sperm-whale—Flower somewhat under-estimated the maximum dimensions.

At what date Flower first began to study whales seriously, it is not easy to ascertain. From the fact of his contributing three papers on this subject to the Zoological Society's *Proceedings* for 1864, it may, however, be inferred that by that time he had devoted no inconsiderable amount of attention to the group. In the first of those he described a specimen of a lesser fin-whale, then recently stranded on the Norfolk coast;

while in a second, and much more important communication, he gave notes on the skeletons of whales preserved in the museums of Holland and Belgium which he had recently visited. Two of these he described as indicating apparently new species; although their right to distinction was not maintained. In the same year he described two skulls of grampuses from Tasmania, which were regarded as representing a new species, under the name of *Orca meridionalis* ; a further note on these being added in the Society's *Proceedings* for 1865, when the species was transferred to the genus *Pseudorca*. Later still it was found that the supposed species was inseparable from the typical *P. crassidens;* námed by Owen many years previously on the evidence of a skeleton from the Lincolnshire Fens. In another note published the same year in the same journal he showed that one of the whales named by him in 1864 was identical with the one now known as *Balæonoptera sibbaldi* ; while a second paper described a specimen of the fin-whale commonly known as *B. musculus*. A further note on the synonymy of *B. sibbaldi* appeared in the *Proceedings* for 1868.

Reverting to earlier publications, in 1866 the Royal Society of London issued a volume containing translations by Flower of certain very important memoirs on Cetacea by Professors Eschricht, Reinhardt, and Lilljeborg. As these were written in a language understood by comparatively few Englishmen, the translation was a distinct benefit to "cetology" in this country.

Between the years 1869 and 1878 inclusive, six very important memoirs on whales (including in that term porpoises, dolphins, etc.) from Flower's pen appeared in the *Transactions* of the Zoological Society of London. The first of these, which was published in the year first mentioned, was devoted to the description of the skeleton of the very interesting and then little-known South American freshwater or estuarine dolphins, *Inia* and *Pontoporia*. In the course of this memoir it was demonstrated that, in spite of the wide distance between their habitats, these dolphins and the freshwater dolphin of the Ganges and certain other Indian rivers, *Platanista gangetica*, collectively form a distinct family group— the Platanistidæ, which exhibits many very generalised features.

In the second memoir of this series, which appeared in 1869, Flower treated in an exhaustive manner of the osteology of the sperm-whale, or cachalot. "The fine skeleton of a young male which he procured for the Museum of the Royal College of Surgeons," writes Professor M'Intosh in his obituary notice of Sir William, "formed the basis of this important paper, and enabled him to add to and correct much which had been written on this subject. The description of its huge cranium as a large, pointed slipper, with a high heel-piece and the front trodden down, the hollow limited behind by the occipital crest, continued laterally into the elevated ridges of the broadly expanded maxillæ, which rose from the median line to the edge of the skull, instead of falling away, as in most Cetaceans, must be familiar to all students of the group. In this vast cavity lies the 'head-matter,' composed of almost pure spermaceti."

It was further demonstrated that the available evidence pointed to the existence of only a single species of true cachalot ; the small adult jaws not unfrequently seen in collections being apparently those of females, which are known to be far inferior in size to the old bulls.

It may be added, in connection with sperm-whales, that the abrupt termination of the muzzle, shown (in a somewhat modified degree) in the model of the old bull, set up under Sir William's direction in the Whale Room at the Natural History Museum, has been said by certain modern naturalists to be incorrect. Inquiries instituted at the present writer's suggestion at the New Bedford Cachalot-whaling Station have, however, proved that the abruptness is under-estimated rather than exaggerated in the restoration.

This brief reference to the Whale Room at the museum, and Flower's work in superintending the construction of models of several of the larger members of the group, must, it may be further added, suffice in this place, seeing that fuller mention of the subiect has been already made in an earlier chapter.

The third memoir of the series in the Zoological Society's *Transactions* treats of the Chinese white dolphin (*Delphinus*, or *Prodelphinus*, *sinensis*), and was published in 1872. In the following year appeared one on Risso's dolphin, *Grampus griseus*, in which the author directed attention to certain variable markings always seen on the skin of this species. These, it has been subsequently shown, are produced by the claws in the suckers of the cuttlefish which forms the food of this species.

The two remaining memoirs in the *Transactions*, which appeared respectively in 1873 and 1878, were devoted to that difficult, and at the time imperfectly known group, termed ziphioid, or beaked whales. In the first of the two attention was concentrated on the aberrant and rare form known as *Berardius arnuxi;* while the second was exclusively devoted to the much more abundant types included under the generic title *Mesoplodon,* in allusion to the single pair of lower teeth near the middle of the sides of the lower jaw, which forms the single dental armature of the cetaceans of this genus. The beaked whales, it should be added, had been previously discussed by Flower in a preliminary paper published in the Zoological Society's *Proceedings* for 1871 and 1876, and likewise in an article communicated in 1872 to *Nature.*

Special interest attaches to a paper by Flower published in the *Transactions* of the Royal Geological Society of Cornwall for 1872, and also in the *Annals and Magazine of Natural History* for the same year, on the bones of a whale dug up at Petuan, in Cornwall, sometime previously to 1829, and now preserved in the museum of the above-named Society. The whale represented by these remains was made the type of the new genus and species *Eschrichtius robustus,* by the late Dr. J. E. Gray. That it was a member of the group of whalebone-whales, and that it could not be identified with either of the genera then known, namely *Balæna, Balænoptera,* and *Megaptera,* was fully demonstrated by Flower, who also showed that it agreed with the two latter in having the neck-vertebræ free.

"The interesting question," he added, "remains, whether this species still exists in our seas; if extinct, it must have become so at a comparatively recent period, certainly long after Cornwall was inhabited by man. The negative evidence of no specimen having been met

K

with by naturalists in a living or recent state, is hardly conclusive as to its non-existence, as our knowledge of this group of animals is lamentably deficient. We are acquainted with many species, even of very large size, only through isolated individuals, and the discovery of others new to science is by no means an infrequent or unlooked-for occurrence at the present time."

In the opinion of the present writer, it is quite probable that this whale may be identical with the grey whale of the Pacific, described many years subsequently by the late Professor Cope as *Rhachianectes glaucus*, in which event that name will have to give place to *Eschrichtius robustus*.

In the year 1879, and for some time after, Flower directed his attention more especially to the dolphins and porpoises, which collectively constitute the family Delphinidæ of naturalists, and he published a series of papers on this group in the *Proceedings* of the Zoological Society. In the volume for 1879 there appeared, for instance, one paper on the common dolphin (*Delphinus delphis*); a second on the bottle-nosed dolphin, now known as *Tursiops tursio*; and a third on the skull of the white whale, or beluga (*Delphinapterus leucas*). Of far greater importance was, however, the appearance in 1883 of a paper in the same serial on the generic characters of the family Delphinidæ as a whole. Special attention was directed in this communication to the value of the pterygoid bones, on the under surface of the skull, in the classification of the family; and characters were formulated which enabled the various genera to be identified, wholly or in part, by this part of the skull. Flower's classification of the Delphinidæ has, with some slight modifications, been very generally accepted by later naturalists. Some time after the publication of this paper the present writer pointed out to the author that two of the generic names employed by him were barred by previous use in a different sense; and in a note subsequently published in the *Proceedings*, these were accordingly replaced.

Flower was, however, by no means forgetful of his earlier love for the cachalot and beaked whales (Physeteridæ); and in 1883 and again in 1884 he published papers in the *Proceedings* on their near relatives the bottle-nosed whales (not to be confounded with the bottle-nosed dolphins) of the genus *Hyperöodon*. In these investigations he was much indebted, as on several previous occasions, to the observations of Captain Gray, a well-known whaler. As regards the common bottle-nose (*H. rostratus*), Sir William succeeded in demonstrating that the great differences which had long been noticed in the skull were due to distinctions either of sex or age; the old males developing huge maxillary crests—with a broad and flattened front surface—of which there is scarcely any trace in the younger members of the same sex, or in females of all ages. In consequence of this difference in the skull, the head of the old bull bottle-nose is easily recognisable by the abrupt and prominent elevation of the forehead immediately behind the base of the beak. Flower was also able to show that bottle-noses yield true spermaceti, especially in the head; a fact which does not appear to have been previously known to zoologists, although it may have been to whalers. At the present day there is a considerable trade in bottle-nose sperm-oil and spermaceti; these being often blended with the products of the cachalot, from which they are distinguishable by their specific gravity. In his 1882 paper Flower described a water-worn bottle-nose skull from Australia, which he regarded as indicating a second species of the genus—*Hyperöodon planifrons*. The correctness of this determination has been demonstrated by complete skeletons of the same whale from the South American seas.

The last two papers on Cetacea by Sir William in the *Proceedings* of the Zoological Society refer to the occurrence of examples of Rudolphi's rorqual (*Balænoptera borealis*) on the English coasts. In the one paper he described a specimen stranded on the Essex shore in 1883, and in the other an example captured in the Thames four years later.

As regards other contributions to our knowledge of the Cetacea, Sir William in 1883 delivered before the Royal Institution a lecture on " Whales, Past and Present," which is reproduced in the *Proceedings* of that body for the same year. A second lecture, " On Whales and Whaling," was delivered before the Royal Colonial Institute for 1885, and is published in the *Journal* of the Institute for that year. The article " Whale," for the ninth edition of the *Encyclopædia Britannica*, is also the work of Flower ; it is reproduced, almost as it stands, in the *Study of Mammals*.

The year 1885 saw the publication of the " List of the Specimens of Cetacea in the Zoological Department of the British Museum," a small, but nevertheless valuable work, from which an extract has already been made. Even when this was written, the museum contained skulls or skeletons of nearly all the more important and well-established representatives of the order, the only notable deficiency being the large whalebone whale from the North Pacific commonly known as the grey whale, and scientifically termed *Rhachianectes glaucus*. It was not many years before this gap was filled by the acquisition of a complete skeleton of the species in question.

In concluding this brief notice of the work accomplished by Flower on the Cetacea, an extract may be made to illustrate his views with regard to the ancestry and origin of the group :—

"The origin of the Cetacea," he wrote, "is at present involved in much obscurity. They present no signs of closer affinity to any of the lower classes of vertebrates than do many other members of their own class. Indeed in all that essentially distinguishes a mammal from the oviparous vertebrates, whether in the osseous, nervous, reproductive, or any other system, they are as truly mammalian as any other group. Any supposed marks of inferiority, as absence of limb-structure, of hairy covering, of lachrymal apparatus, etc., are obviously modifications (or degradations, as they may be termed) in adaptation to their special mode of life. The characters of the teeth of *Zeuglodon* and other extinct forms, and also of the fœtal Mystacocetes, clearly indicate that they have been derived from mammals in which the heterodont type of dentition was fully established. The steps by which a land mammal may have been modified into a purely aquatic one are indicated by the stages which still survive among the Carnivora in the Otariidæ and in the true seals. A further change in the same direction would produce an animal somewhat resembling a dolphin; and it has been thought that this may have been the route by which the Cetacean form has been developed. There are, however, great difficulties in the way of this view. Thus if the hind-limbs had ever been developed into the very efficient aquatic propelling organs they present in the seals, it is not easy to imagine how they could have become completely atrophied and their function transferred to the tail. So that, from this point of view, it is more likely that whales were derived from animals with long tails, which were used in swimming, eventually with such effect that the hind-limbs became no longer necessary. The powerful tail, with its lateral cutaneous flanges, of an American species of otter (*Lutra brasiliensis*) may give an idea of this member in the primitive Cetaceans. But the structure of the Cetacea is, in so many essential characters, so unlike that of the Carnivora, that the probabilities are against these orders being nearly related. Even in the skull of the *Zeuglodon*, which has been cited as presenting a great resemblance to that of a seal, quite as many likenesses may be traced to one of the primitive Pig-like Ungulates (except in the purely adaptive character of the form of the teeth) while the elongated larynx, complex stomach, simple liver, reproductive organs, both male and female, and fœtal membranes of the existing Cetacea, are far more like those of that group than of the Carnivora. Indeed, it appears probable that the old popular idea which affixed the name of ʻSea-Hogʼ to the porpoise, contains a larger element of truth than the speculations of many accomplished zoologists of modern times. The fact that *Platanista*, which, as mentioned above, appears to retain more of the primitive characteristics of the group than any other existing form, and also the distantly related *Inia* from South America, are both at the present day exclusively fluviatile, may point to the fresh-water origin of the whole group, in which case their otherwise rather inexplicable absence from the seas of the Cretaceous period would be accounted for.

" On the other hand, it should be observed that the teeth of the Zeuglodonts approximate more to a carnivorous than to an ungulate type."

This difficulty with regard to the teeth is indeed one which it is impossible to disregard, since it is scarcely credible that grinding teeth such as characterise herbivorous mammals of all descriptions could ever have been modified into the teeth of whales, either living or extinct. There is, moreover, the unmistakable resemblance presented by the cheek-teeth of the aforesaid extinct zeuglodons to those of Carnivora. Both these facts seem to point to the derivation of toothed whales, at any rate, from flesh-eating rather than herbivorous mammals ; although they have certainly no relationship with the eared seals.

Since the foregoing passage was written it has been practically demonstrated that the toothed whales, at any rate, are the descendants of primitive Carnivora. Professor E. Fraas, of Stuttgart, and Dr. C. W. Andrews, of the British Museum, have, for instance, shown that the zeuglodons are derived from the Eocene group of Carnivora known as Creodontia ; while there is every reason for regarding the zeuglodons themselves as the ancestors of modern toothed whales.

CHAPTER VII

ANTHROPOLOGICAL WORK

THE study of the physical characters of the various native races of the human species—that is to say, anthropology, in contradistinction to ethnology—occupied a very prominent position in Sir William Flower's scientific career; and it is difficult to say whether this or the study of whales was the branch of biology on which his greatest interest was concentrated. Perhaps we might say that the two together formed his especially favourite subjects. Whereas, however, as we have seen in the last chapter, he was studying the Cetacea at least as early as the year 1864, when papers from his pen were published, anthropology does not appear to have been seriously taken up by him till considerably later in life; the first papers and lectures by him that have come under the writer's notice dating from 1878.

As regards the special departments of this science to which Sir William devoted a large share of attention, we may mention, in the first place, the discovery of the best methods of accurately determining the capacity of the human cranium, and the drawing-up of formulæ for "indexes" to serve as a basis for comparing the cranial measurements of different races. Secondly, we may take the classification of these races as one of his most important lines of investigation. While, in the third place, may be noticed his partiality for the study of the inferior races of mankind, more especially those belonging to the black, or Negro, branch of the species ; dwarf races, like the Central African Akkas, and the Andaman Islanders, or exterminated types, like the Tasmanians, having apparently a very strong claim on his interest. And here it may be mentioned that not only is anthropology largely indebted to Flower for his published works on this subject, but likewise for the energy he displayed in collecting specimens of the osteology of dwindling races, while there was yet time. It was at his initiation that Sir Joseph Fayrer was induced to use his influence with the Indian authorities for the purpose of securing skulls and skeletons of Andamanese for the Museum of the Royal College of Surgeons. The result of this was the acquisition of a fine series of specimens of the osteology of this fast-disappearing race, at a time when it was still comparatively uncontaminated and undeteriorated by contact with Europeans. That such contact must inevitably lead, sooner or later, to the disappearance of the inferior, or " non-adaptive " races of mankind, was a favourite dictum of Sir William's ; and its truth has been confirmed by the events of the last few years.

If not actually the earliest, the first really important contribution to anthropology on Flower's part was a Friday Evening lecture " On the Native Races of the Pacific Ocean," delivered at the Royal Institution on 31st May 1878, and published in the *Proceedings* of that body for the same year. In this lecture Sir William described the native races of Oceania, or those inhabiting the islands, inclusive of Australia, scattered through the great ocean tract bounded on the east and west respectively by the continents of America and Asia. The subject was treated very largely upon the basis of the collection of skulls and skeletons in the Museum of the Royal College of Surgeons; yet the lecturer was careful to point out that even this extensive series was wholly insufficient for the purpose of forming a classification of mankind founded on physical structure.

"It can only afford certain indications, valuable as far as they go, from which a provisional, or approximative system may be built up. Very many, indeed the majority of the islands, are totally unrepresented in it; others are illustrated by only one or two individuals." "Were the collection anything like representative," it is added later, "it would probably be found possible to distinguish the natives of each island, or, at all events, of each group of islands, by cranial characters alone."

Special attention was in this course directed to the Australians on the one hand, and to the frizzly-haired Melanesians, or Oceanic Negroes (as distinct from the straight-haired Polynesians) on the other. That the Melanesians were the primitive denizens of the greater part of Oceania, and that the original area they once inhabited has been much circumscribed by Polynesian invasion, the lecturer was fully convinced; and the great difficulty of distinguishing in some instances to what extent this invasion has led, in certain cases, to a mixture of the two stocks, was earnestly insisted upon. At the conclusion of his discourse Flower commented very strongly on the urgent need of making anthropological collections in these islands forthwith; and, although perhaps his prophecy of impending extermination was a little exaggerated, it is no less urgent at the present day.

"In another half century," he said, "the Australians, the Melanesians, the Maories, and most of the Polynesians will have followed the Tasmanians to the grave. We shall well merit the reproach of future generations if we neglect our present opportunities of gathering together every fragment of knowledge that can still be saved, of their languages, customs, social polity, manufactures, and arts. The preservation of tangible evidence of their physical structure is, if possible, still more important; and surely this may be expected of that nation, above all others, which by its commercial enterprise and wide-spread maritime dominion has done, and is doing, far more than any in effecting that distinctive revolution."

What are we doing at the present day, it may be asked, to avoid this reproach? If we may judge by the slowness with which anthropological specimens came into the national collections (and it is difficult to select a better test), the answer must surely be, I am afraid, in the negative.

Of a still more popular type than the preceding was a lecture on the "Races of Men," delivered by Flower in the City Hall, Glasgow, on 28th November 1878, and published as a separate pamphlet.

The third, and perhaps the most interesting lecture given by Flower during the year under consideration, was the one at Manchester on November 30th, on the "Aborigines of Tasmania," which is published in the tenth series of *Manchester Science Lectures*. In this discourse Flower traced the sad story of European intercourse with this interesting people and their final extermination ; pointing out that the last male died in 1869, and the last female in 1876. At the time this lecture was delivered four complete skeletons of Tasmanians of both sexes had been obtained and sent to England by the late Mr. Merton Allport, of Hobart. Of these, two were then in the museum of the Royal College of Surgeons, while the third was in the collection of the late Dr. Barnard Davis, and the fourth in that of the Anthropological Institute of London. Dr. Davis's specimen came to the Museum of the College of Surgeons after the owner's death; and it was a great source of satisfaction to Sir William that, in after years, he obtained the Anthropological Institute's specimen (which is remarkable for retaining the interfrontal suture of the skull) for the Natural History Museum. Somewhat less than thirty Tasmanian skulls were at this time known to exist in England, and a few have been since acquired for public collections. Flower dwelt upon the close affinity of the Tasmanians to the Melanesians (although the skulls of the two are perfectly distinguishable), and their wide difference from their Australian neighbours.

Perhaps, however, the most important contribution made by Flower to anthropology in 1878 was his paper on the " Methods and Results of Measurements of the Capacity of Human Crania," which appeared in the *Report* of the British Association for that year and also in *Nature*.

This was paving the way for the first part of the valuable " Catalogue of Osteological Specimens in the Museum of the Royal College of Surgeons of England," which appeared in the following year, and is entirely devoted to man. This accurate and laborious work was very far from being a mere catalogue of the contents of this section of the museum under the author's charge, for it is in fact to a great extent a manual of the methods employed in human craniology; tables and figures being given of the manner in which the measurement of skulls are made, and the method of calculating "cranial indexes." For taking the cubical capacity of skulls Flower employed mustard seed, and the "craniometer" invented by Mr. Busk. In the introduction is given a general sketch of the osteology of man, followed by a dissertation on his dentition, and this, in turn, by an account of the special osteological and dental features of the various native races of the human species.

Earlier in the same year Flower had entered in some degree on the domain of ethnology by contributing to the *Journal* of the Anthropological Institute a paper illustrating the "Mode of Preserving the Dead in Darnley Island and in South Australia," figuring the mummified body of a Melanesian from the above-named island. Another paper of somewhat similar nature from Flower's pen was published in the same journal for 1881, dealing with a collection of monu-mental heads and artificially deformed crania of Melanesians from the Island of Mallicollo, in the New Hebrides. These preserved heads have attracted the attention of Europeans ever since Cook's visit to the island in 1774; and appear to be quite unique.

"Whatever the special motive among the Malli-collese," wrote Flower, "whether they are the objects of worship or merely of affectionate regard, it must be very difficult for a passing traveller without intimate knowledge of the language and of the condition of mind and thought of the people to ascertain ; but the custom is obviously analogous to many others which have prevailed throughout all historical times and in many nations, manifesting itself among other forms in the mummified bodies of the ancient Egyptians, and which has received its most æsthetic expression in the marble busts placed over the mouldering bones in a Christian cathedral."

Reverting to 1879, we find in the *Journal* of the Anthropological Institute for that year an important and interesting paper by Flower on the "Osteology and Affinities of the Natives of the Andaman Islands," a subject to which the author made a further contribution in the same journal for November 1884. In the first of these communications the author gave the results of the examination of nineteen skeletons and a large series of skulls, while in the second he was able to amplify these, and thus to render his averages more trustworthy by the details of no less than ten additional skeletons. As in all his other papers of this nature, Sir William first traced in considerable detail the history of European intercourse with the Andamanese, or " Mincopies," as they were often called at one time, and then proceeded to point out the external and osteological features of these interesting and diminutive people. Relying to a great extent on the "frizzly," or "woolly" character of their hair, Flower was fully convinced that these people belong to the Negro branch of the human family.

"With the Oceanic Negroes, or Melanesians, as they are now commonly called, we might naturally suppose they had the most in common. But this is not the case. Although the Melanesians vary much in stature, none are so small as the Andamanese, and some are fully equal to the average of the species. Their crania, whenever they are met with in a pure state, are remarkably long, narrow, and high. . . . The pure Fijians are perhaps the most dolichocephalic [long-headed] race in the world, and the New Caledonians and the New Hebrideans come near them. In this respect they are therefore as distinct as possible from the Andamanese. . . . As is well known, the African frizzly-haired races are mostly of moderate or tall stature, but there are among them some, as the Bushmen of the South, and others less known from the Central regions, as diminutive as the Andamanese."

The lecturer then went on to state that although African Negroes were, as a rule, of the long-headed type, yet there were even then indications of the existence of round-headed races in the heart of the continent. In conclusion, it was added that although their very rounded skulls probably formed a special feature of the Andamanese, yet that he regarded the " Negritos," or group of which that race formed a section, "as representing an infantile, undeveloped or primitive form of the type from which the African Negroes on the one hand, and the Melanesians on the other, with all their various modifications, may have sprung. Even their very geographical position, in the centre of the great area of distribution of the frizzly-haired races, seems to favour this view. We may, therefore, regard them as little-modified descendants of an extremely ancient race, the ancestors of all the Negro tribes."

On the other hand, it was suggested that long isolation and restriction to a confined area might have led to physical degeneration, so that the peculiarities of the Andamanese type might be of comparatively recent origin.

Another interesting race to which Sir William devoted special attention was the Fijians, who, as already incidentally mentioned, offer the most extreme contrast to the round-headed Andamanese, by the extreme length and narrowness of their skulls. His paper on the "Cranial Characters of the Natives of the Fiji Islands," appeared in the *Journal* of the Anthropological Institute for 1880 ; and was illustrated, like the one on the Andamanese, with carefully drawn figures of typical skulls. After mentioning that nothing definite was known with regard to the anthropology of one of the islands of the Fiji, or Viti, group, the author added that "with regard to Viti Levu, all the evidence we possess shows that the people who inhabit the interior of the island present in their cranial conformation a remarkable purity of type, and that this type conforms in the main with that of the Melanesian islands generally ; indeed they may be regarded as the most characteristic, almost exaggerated, expressions of this type, for in ' hypersistenocephaly ' (extreme narrowness of skull), they exceed the natives of Fati, in the New Hebrides, to which the term was first applied.

" The intermixture of Tongans or other Polynesian blood with the Fijian, appears to be confined to the smaller islands, and even in these not to have very greatly modified the prevailing cranial characteristics."

At the meeting of the British Association for the Advancement of Science, held at York in the autumn of 1881, Professor Flower, as Chairman of the Department, read an address to the Anthropological Department on the study and progress of anthropology, more especially in this country; at the conclusion of which he urged the strong claim of the Anthropological Institute of Great Britain and Ireland to the support of all interested in that subject. Three years later (1884) he gave, as President, an address "On the Aims and Prospects of the Study of Anthropology," before the last-named body, at the Anniversary Meeting in January. Here again the speaker directed attention to the comparatively small degree of interest taken in this country in this most important science, and urged that not only scientific students, but wealthy men, ought to do something towards aiding its progress. "Our insular position, maritime supremacy, numerous dependencies, and ramifying commerce, have given us," he remarked, "unusually favourable opportunities for the formation of such collections—opportunities which, unfortunately, in past times have not been used so fully as might be desired." A change, indeed, it was added, had of late years come over matters in this respect; but, while fully admitting this, it can scarcely be maintained that even at the present day we are doing all that we might in this direction.

Between the years 1879 and 1885 inclusive, Flower appears to have devoted much of his attention to elaborating a satisfactory biological classification of the various races of mankind. In the former he drew up a preliminary scheme of this nature, which was published in the *British Medical Journal* for 1879 and 1880, under the title of " Anatomical Characters of the Races of Man." Impressed with the importance of having some well-marked feature, other than those afforded by the skull, by means of which the skeletons of such races could easily be distinguished, he turned his attention to the scapula, or shoulder-blade, and in 1880, with the assistance of Dr. J. G. Garson, published in the *Journal of Anatomy and Physiology* a paper " On the Scapular Index as a Race-Character in Man." On the whole, although the number of skeletons examined was confessedly insufficient, the results obtained were decidedly satisfactory, and agreed fairly well with those of other observers. The Australians and Andamanese, for instance, accorded in this respect with the Negro type. On the other hand, Bushman skeletons, as had been observed in Paris, approached in this respect to the Caucasian type, while the Tasmanians were unexpectedly found to differ markedly from the other black races in their scapular index.

In 1884, in a paper published in the *Journal* of the Anthropological Society, Sir William recorded the results of a large series of observations in regard to the value of the size of the teeth as a race-character, and was enabled, by means of a " dental index," to divide the human species into a " Microdont," or small-toothed group, a " Mesodont " group and a " Macrodont," or large-toothed group. In the first group were included Europeans and other members of the Caucasian stock, as well as Polynesians, and many of the non-Aryan tribes of Central and Southern India. In the second group came Chinese, American Indians, Malays, and African Negroes; while in the third were included Melanesians, Andamanese, Australians, and Tasmanians. If ·it be borne in mind, as explained in the original paper, that the teeth in African Negroes are actually larger than in Europeans, although the "index" is reduced by the great length of the base of the cranium (which forms a factor in the index) in the former, the results accord remarkably well with the under-mentioned classification of the human species, which is indeed partly based on the character in question.

"The Classification of the Varieties of the Human Species" is the title of Flower's Presidential Address to the Anniversary Meeting of the Anthropological Institute, held in January 1885. In this scheme the species was divided into three main stocks, or branches, namely (1) the Negroid, or black; (2) the Mongolian, or yellow; and (3) the Caucasian, or white. In the first were included the African or typical Negroes, the Hottentots and Bushmen, the Oceanic Negroes or Melanesians, and the Negritos of the Andaman Islands and other parts of Asia; the Australians being provisionally classed near the Melanesians. The second, or Mongolian, branch was taken to include the Eskimo, the typical Mongols of Central and Northern Asia, the brown Polynesians or "Kanakas," and the so-called American Indians, from the great lakes of Canada to Patagonia and Tierra del Fuego. In the third, or Caucasian, group were classed, of course, all the remaining representatives of the human race, including Europeans, the ancient Egyptians, and the modern fellahin of the Nile delta, the natives of India, the Ainu of Japan, and the Veddas of Ceylon.

In the main, this classification has been very generally accepted by anthropologists, although exception has naturally been taken to some of the items. The Australians, for instance, which differ markedly from all the undoubted representatives of the Negroid branch, form a case in point. Sir William was inclined to think that these people do not form a distinct race at all, but that they may be derived from a Melanesian stock, modified by a strong infusion of some other race, probably a low Caucasian type, more or less nearly allied to the Veddas of Ceylon or some of the Dravidian races of Southern or Central India. It is added, however, that the Australians may possibly be mainly sprung from a very primitive type, from which the frizzly-haired Negroes branched off; frizzly hair being probably a specialised feature not the common attribute of the ancestral man; confirmation of this last supposition being afforded, it may be mentioned, by the straight hair of the man-like apes.

Neither of the above theories is, however, altogether satisfactory; and it has been suggested by some writers that the Australians, like the Veddas of Ceylon, and the Indian Dravidians, are a very primitive Caucasian type. Against this, is their scapular index, their large teeth, and projecting jaws (which must not be confused with protrusion of the lips alone). Until, however, we know which of the three great human branches was the one which traces its origin back to ape-like creatures, it is almost impossible to arrive at any satisfactory conclusion on this puzzling question.

Another point in regard to which Flower's classification has met with adverse criticism is the position assigned to the brown Polynesians, which some authorities believe to be mainly of Caucasian origin, and accordingly term Indonesians.

Taken as a whole there can, however, be no question but that the classification proposed by Sir William was an extremely valuable contribution to systematic anthropology.

The last two really important contributions to anthropology made by Sir William were both published in 1888 : the one, under the title of " The Pygmy Races of Man," in the *Proceedings* of the Royal Institution (forming an address); and the other, entitled " Description of Two Skeletons of Akkas, a Pygmy Race from Central Africa," in the *Journal* of the Anthropological Institute. The second of these two communications dealt with two imperfect skeletons—male and female—of the pigmy African race known as Akkas, obtained by the late Dr. Emin Pasha at Monbotto during his last expedition. The female specimen, which is the least imperfect of the two, and is said to be that of a very old individual, is now mounted in the Natural History Museum. In general character, the skulls were found to come very close to the Negro type; it is true they are somewhat less elongated, but the relative breadth proved to be much less than the describer was led to expect from what had been previously written with regard to the craniology of this tribe. The whole skeleton fully confirmed earlier statements that the Akkas are the most diminutive living people. They are quite distinct from the African Bushmen (characterised, among other features, by their tawny skins), and also from the Asiatic Negritos, as represented by the Andamanese ; and they accordingly seem rightly referred to a distinct branch of the Negro stock, for which the name Negrillo has been suggested.

In the first of the two papers cited above, Sir William gave a general account of all the races of mankind which can be included under the title of " pigmies," such as the Bushmen, Negrillos, and Negritos. As regards the second group he wrote as follows :—

" The fact now seems clearly demonstrated that at various spots across the great African Continent, within a few degrees north and south of the Equator, extending from the Atlantic coast to near the shores of the Albert Nyanza (30° E. long.) and perhaps . . . even further to the east, south of the Galla land, are still surviving, in scattered districts, communities of these small Negroes, all much resembling each other in size, appearance, and habits, and dwelling mostly apart from their taller neighbours, by whom they are everywhere surrounded. . . . In many parts, especially at the west, they are obviously holding their own with difficulty, if not actually disappearing, and there is much about their condition of civilisation, and the situations in which they are found, to induce us to look upon them, as in the case of the Bushmen in the south and the Negritos in the east, as the remains of a population which occupied the land before the incoming of the present dominant races. If the account of the

Nasamenians, related by Herodotus, be accepted as historical, the river they came to, 'flowing from west to east,' must have been the Niger, and the northward range of the dwarfish people far more extensive twenty-three centuries ago than it is at the present time."

Sir William's only remaining anthropological paper of any importance appears to be one on skulls of the aboriginal natives of Jamaica, published in the *Journal* of the Anthropological Institute for 1890.

It should not, however, be forgotten that, as more fully narrated in an earlier chapter, one of the last acts of Sir William's scientific career was to organise the arrangement of the anthropological series in the Natural History Branch of the British Museum—an undertaking of which he was not spared to witness the completion (so far as anything of this nature can be said to be anywhere near " complete ").

If he had left nothing but his anthropological labours to bear testimony to his zeal for science and his capacity for organisation, Sir William Flower would have deserved well of posterity. And it should be recorded to his credit that the majority of naturalists, at all events in this country, are employing, with some minor modifications, not only his anthropological classification, but that of mammals in general. It is true that both these schemes were based on the labours and ideas of his predecessors, but it was reserved for him to so modify and improve them as to lead to the almost universal acceptation with which they have been received.

CHAPTER VIII

MUSEUM AND MISCELLANEOUS WORK

MUCH of the substance of this chapter has been already alluded to in the earlier portions of the present volume ; but it has been found convenient to give Sir William's views on the objects and arrangement of museums somewhat more fully in this place, while reference is also made to various items of miscellaneous work which do not fall within the scope of either of the three previous chapters.

Of Flower's hereditary interest in the crusade against tight bearing-reins, and his official connection with the Anti-Bearing-Rein Association, sufficient mention has been already made in the first chapter. It will likewise be unnecessary in this place to do more than mention his *Diagrams of the Nerves of the Human Body* published in 1861, to his " Supplement to the Catalogue of the Pathological Series in the Museum of the Royal College of Surgeons," issued in 1863, and to certain articles on surgical subjects contributed by him at an early portion of his career. All these, coupled with the practical experience he gained during his Crimean service, indicate, however, that had Sir William decided to devote his energies and talents to surgery as a permanent occupation, there is little doubt he would have risen to high eminence in that profession.

The little work entitled *Fashion in Deformity*, is based

on a Friday Evening lecture at the Royal Institution, delivered on 7th May 1880, and first published in the *Proceedings* of the Institution for the same year. In its separate, and more fully illustrated form, it was issued in 1881. This is certainly one of Flower's most original efforts, touching upon ground much of which has received but little notice from either earlier or later writers. The subjects discussed include the origin of fashion; mutilations of domesticated animals by man for the sake of fashion; fashion in hair and in finger-nails; tattooing; fashion in noses, ears, lips, teeth, and head, the latter being illustrated by the curious custom prevalent among certain widely sundered races of forcibly compressing the cranium in infancy by means of bandages, so as to permanently modify and alter its contour to a greater or less degree. Analogous to this compression of the head is the crippling by bandages of the feet of Chinese female infants, which is described in some detail. But the author is of opinion that European nations are scarcely less to blame in the matter of distorting the feet for the sake of fashion; and pointed-toed and high-heeled boots and shoes come in for his most severe condemnation. Neither, as mentioned in the first chapter, was he less scathing in his diatribes against the corset and tight-lacing. That the last-mentioned article of female attire is likewise charged in certain instances with being the inducing cause of cancer was however probably unknown to him.

That these strictures against the prevalent fashions of our own days had little or no practical result (certainly none in the case of the female sex), may be taken for granted. The work has, however, a very considerable amount of interest as illustrating a number of instances of the manner in which uncivilised nations modify and mutilate various parts of the body for the sake of what they are pleased to regard as ornament, or fashion ; and is therefore a valuable contribution to ethnology.

The address delivered by Flower at the meeting of the Church Congress, held at Reading in 1883, on the bearing of recent scientific advances on the Christian faith, has likewise been alluded to in the first chapter. It will therefore suffice here to quote a portion of the concluding paragraph, which demonstrates that nothing among modern discoveries had served to shake in the very slightest degree the author's profound belief in all the essential truths of the faith of his forefathers.

" Science," he observes, " has thrown some light, little enough at present, but ever increasing, and for which we should all be thankful, upon the processes or methods by which the world in which we dwell has been brought into its present condition. The wonder and mystery of Creation remain as wonderful and mysterious as before. Of the origin of the whole, science tells us nothing. It is still as impossible as ever to conceive that such a world, governed by laws, the operations of which have led to such mighty results, and are attended by such future promise, could have originated without the intervention of some power external to itself. If the succession of small miracles, supposed to regulate the operations of nature, no longer satisfies us, have we not substituted for them one of immeasurable greatness and grandeur ? "

Although he does not say so in so many words, there is little doubt (reading between the lines) that Flower regarded the evolution of animated Nature as part of a preordained divine plan, and that he had little, if any, faith in such theories as "survival of the fittest," as the true explanation of Nature's riddle.

This address, like most of the other addresses and papers discussed in this chapter, is reprinted in *Essays on Museums*.

We pass now to the concluding portion of our subject, namely Flower's influence and example in modifying and advancing previous conceptions as to the functions and objects of museums, and the mode and manner in which their contents should be arranged and distributed : on the one hand for the purpose of instructing and interesting the public, and on the other for advancing the study of biological science. In many respects this was perhaps the most important item in Flower's life-work ; and he may be said to have created the art of museum development and display.

In regard to the value and importance of his labours in this respect, no better testimony can be adduced than that given by such a distinguished adept in this kind of work as Professor E. Ray Lankester, the present Director of the Natural History Departments of the British Museum.

"The arrangement and exhibition of specimens designed and carried out by Flower in both instances," writes Professor Lankester, after alluding to his predecessor's labours first at the Royal College of Surgeons, and afterwards at the British Museum, "was so definite an improvement on previous methods, that he deserves to be considered as an originator and inventor in museum work. His methods have not only met with general approval, and their application with admiration, but they have been largely adapted and copied by other Curators and Directors of public museums both at home and abroad."

Much has been said with regard to Flower's views on museum arrangement in the chapter devoted to his official connection with the British Museum. It may, however, be permissible to repeat that in his epoch-making address on museum organisation, delivered before the British Association in 1889, he insisted, in the case of large central public museums, on the absolute necessity of separating the study from the exhibition series ; and likewise on the limited number and careful selection of the specimens which should be shown to the public in the latter, and the prime importance of carefully-written and simply-worded descriptive labels for each group of specimens, if not, indeed, for each individual specimen. His idea was, in fact, that the specimens should illustrate the labels rather than the labels the specimens. A limited number, rather than an extensive series, of exhibited specimens, and ample room for each, were also features in his progress of reform. Not less emphatic was Sir William on the importance of combining the extinct with the living forms in our museums; but this, as stated elsewhere, he was unable to carry out in the national collection.

It was, however, by no means only in our great national museums that Flower took so much interest, and advocated (and to a great extent succeeded in

carrying out) such sweeping and beneficial changes.
He was equally convinced of the supreme importance
and value, as educating media, of school and county
museums, if organised and kept up on proper and
rational lines ; and he did all that lay in his power to
promote the establishment, extension, or development
of institutions of this nature.

At the request of the Head-Master, in 1889, Flower
furnished some written advice as to the best method of
arranging a museum at Eton College, and these were
published as an article in *Nature* for that year, under
the title of " School Museums." The writer observed
that the subjects best adapted for such a museum are
zoology, botany, mineralogy, and geology ; adding
that " everything in the museum should have some
distinct object, coming under one or other of the
above subjects, and under one or other of the series
defined below, and everything else should be rigorously
excluded. The Curator's business will be quite as much
to keep useless specimens out of the museum as to
acquire those that are useful." It was further urged that
the " Index Museum," in the Natural History Museum,
furnished the best guide to the lines on which a school
museum should be furnished and arranged, but that the
exhibits should be restricted to a simpler and less
detailed series.

Under the title of " Natural History as a Vocation,"
Sir William published in *Chambers' Journal* for April
1897 an article dealing with biology as a profession, and
also discussing the best means of encouraging and
directing the " collecting instinct," which is so marked
a feature in some boys. This article is reprinted

in *Essays on Museums*, under the title of "Boys' Museums." It serves to show that Flower considered the aforesaid "collecting instinct" worthy, under certain restrictions, of every encouragement.

Since the appearance of Flower's article pointing out their value and importance, natural history museums have been established at many, if not most, of our public schools besides Eton. Those at Marlborough, Rugby, and Haileybury may be specially noticed as being, to a great extent, arranged on the lines advocated by Sir William.

As regards county and other local museums, Flower in the article under the latter title, published in *Essays on Museums*, advocated that these, in addition to natural history specimens, should likewise illustrate the archæology, and indeed the general history of the district ; obsolete implements, such as flint-and-steel and candle-snuffers, if of local origin, legitimately finding a place within its walls. The natural history of the locality, needless to say, should be well illustrated, and so arranged and named that any visitor can easily identify every creature and plant he may have met with during his rambles in the district.

The subject of administration is next discussed, when after fully admitting the value of volunteer assistance, the writer lays it down as imperative that a competent paid Curator must be engaged if the museum is to be really useful and to properly fulfil its purpose.

Now that so many institutions of this nature are under the control of the County Councils, and their expenses defrayed out of the rates, the following passage has a most important bearing on the management of local museums :—

"The scope of the museum," observes Sir William, "should be strictly defined and limited ; there must be nothing like the general miscellaneous collection of 'curiosities,' thrown indiscriminately together, which constituted the old-fashioned country museum. I think we are all agreed as to the local character predominating. One section should contain antiquities and illustrations of local manners and customs ; another section, local natural history, zoology, botany, and geology. The boundaries of the county will afford a good limit for both. Everything not occurring in a state of nature within that boundary should be rigorously excluded. In addition to this, it may be desirable to have a small general collection designed and arranged specially for elementary instruction in science."

These words of warning deserve, in the present writer's opinion, more attention than they have yet received at the hands of those responsible for the administration of not a few local museums.

It may be added that Flower was of opinion that ordinary local museums should not undertake original research work, which should be reserved for the larger establishments in our chief cities and the metropolis. With the means at their disposal—often insufficient even for the proper functions—local museums should have quite enough to do in illustrating local products.

Not that Sir William Flower was of opinion that, in our larger cities, museums of a totally different nature from the local museum on the one hand and from the general museum on the other, may not have a justifiable *locus standi*. This is amply demonstrated by his remarks (republished in *Essays on Museums*) on the occasion of the opening of the Booth Museum at Brighton, in November 1890, which contains one of the finest and best mounted collection of British birds in the kingdom.

M

APPENDIX A

SOME BIOGRAPHICAL AND OBITUARY NOTICES OF SIR WILLIAM FLOWER.

The Biograph and Review, vol. vi. No. 31 (1881).
Medical News, 16th December 1881.
Contemporary Medical Men. London, 1887.
The *Times,* 3rd July 1899.
The *Spectator,* July 1899.
Nature, 13th July 1889. Professor E. R. Lankester.
Natural Science, August 1899. R. Lydekker.
Geological Magazine, August 1899. Dr. H. Woodward.
Scottish Review, April 1900. Professor M'Intosh.
" Year-book " of the Royal Society, 1901. W. C. M.
"Sir William Henry Flower, K.C.B. ; A Personal Memoir." By C. J. Cornish. London, 1904.

APPENDIX B

LIST OF THE MORE IMPORTANT SCIENTIFIC PUBLICATIONS OF SIR WILLIAM FLOWER.

A. BOOKS AND SEPARATE PAMPHLETS.

1. "Diagrams of the Nerves of the Human Body, Exhibiting their Origin, Divisions, and Connections." London, 1861.

2. "A Supplement to the Catalogue of the Pathological Series in the Museum of the Royal College of Surgeons." London, 1863.

3. "Introductory Lectures to the Course of Comparative Anatomy, delivered at the Royal College of Surgeons of England, 1870." London, 1870.

4. " An Introduction to the Osteology of the Mammalia," being the substance of the course of lectures delivered at the Royal College of Surgeons of England in 1870. London, 1870. Second edition, 1876. Third edition (revised with the assistance of Hans Gadow), 1885.

5. " Catalogue of the Specimens illustrating the Osteology and Dentition of Vertebrated Animals, Recent and Extinct, contained in the Museum of the Royal College of Surgeons of England." London. Part I. Man (1879); Part II. Mammalia (1884), written in conjunction with Dr. J. G. Garson.

6. " Fashion in Deformity, as Illustrated in the Customs of Barbarous and Civilised Races." (*Nature* series). London, 1881. Also published in the *Proceedings* of the Royal Institution for 1880.

7. " Recent Advances in Natural Science, in their Relation to the Christian Faith." A paper read before the Church Congress, 1885. London, 1885.

8. " Recent Memoirs on the Cetacea," by Eschricht, Reinhardt, and Liljeborg. A Translation. London (Ray Society), 1866.

9. " List of the Specimens of Cetacea in the Zoological Department of the British Museum." London, 1885.

10. " An Introduction to the Study of Mammals Living and Extinct " (written in collaboration with R. Lydekker). London, 1891.

11. " The Horse: a Study in Natural History." London, 1891.

12. " Essays on Museums and Other Subjects connected with Natural History." London, 1898.

B. Zoological and Anatomical Memoirs, Articles, and Notes published in Scientific Serials, etc.

a. In the " Philosophical Transactions " of the Royal Society of London.

13. " Observations on the Posterior Lobes of the Cerebrum of the Quadrumana, with the Description of the

Brain of a Galago," vol. clii. pp. 185-201 (1862). Abstract in *Proc. Roy. Soc.*, vol. xi. pp. 376-381 (1860).

14. "On the Commissures of the Cerebral Hemispheres of the Marsupialia and Monotremata, as compared with those of the Placental Mammals," vol. clv. pp. 633-651 (1865). Abstract in *Proc. Roy. Soc.*, vol. xiv. pp. 71-74 (1865.)

15. "On the Development and Succession of the Teeth in the Marsupialia," vol. clvii. pp. 631-642 (1867). Abstract in *Proc. Roy. Soc.*, vol. xv. pp. 464-468 (1867), and in *Ann. Mag. Nat. Hist.*, vol. xx. pp. 129-133 (1867.)

16. "On a Newly-discovered Extinct Mammal from Patagonia (*Homalodontotherium cunninghami*)," vol. clxiv. pp. 173-182 (1874). Abstract in *Proc. Roy. Soc.*, vol. xxi. p. 383 (1873).

17. "Seals and Cetaceans from Kerguelen Island (*Transit of Venus Expeditions*, 1874 and 1875)," vol. clxviii. pp. 95-100 (1876).

b. In the " Proceedings " of the Royal Society of London.

18. Reply to Professor Owen's paper : "On Zoological Names of Characteristic Parts and Homological Interpretations and Beginnings, especially in reference to Connecting Fibres of the Brain," vol. xiv. pp. 134-139 (1865).

c. In the " Transactions " of the Zoological Society of London.

19. "On the Brain of the Javan Loris (*Stenops javanicus*, Illig.)," vol. v. pp. 103-111 (1866).

20. "Description of the Skeleton of *Inia geoffroyensis*, and of the Skull of *Pontoporia blainvillei*," vol. vi. pp. 87-116 (1869).

21. "On the Osteology of the Sperm-Whale or Cachalot (*Physeter macrocephalus*)," vol. vi. pp 309-372 (1869).

22. "Description of the Skeleton of the Chinese White Dolphin (*Delphinus sinensis*)," vol. vii. pp. 151-160 (1872).

23. "On Risso's Dolphin (*Grampus griseus*)," vol. viii. pp. 1-21 (1873).

24. "On the Recent Ziphioid Whales, with a Description

of the Skeleton of *Berardius arnuxi*," vol. viii. pp. 203-234 (1873).

25. "A Further Contribution to the Knowledge of the Existing Ziphioid Whales; Genus *Mesoplodon*," vol. x. pp. 415-437 (1878).

d. In the " Proceedings " of the Zoological Society of London.

26. "Notes on the Dissection of a Species of Galago," 1852, pp. 73-75.

27. "On the Structure of the Gizzard of the Nicobar Pigeon and Granivorous Birds," 1860, pp. 330-334.

28. "Notes on the Anatomy of *Pithecia monachus*, Geoffr.," 1862, pp. 326-333.

29. "On the Optic Lobes of the Brain of the *Echidna*," 1864, pp. 18-20.

30. "On a Lesser Fin-Whale (*Balænoptera rostrata*, Fabr.) recently stranded on the Norfolk Coast," 1864, pp. 252-258.

31. "On the Brain of the Red Howling Monkey (*Mycetes seniculus*, Linn.)," 1864, pp. 335-338.

32. "Notes on the Skeletons of Whales in the Principal Museums of Holland and Belgium, with Descriptions of Two Species, apparently new to Science (*Sibbaldius schlegeli* and *Physalus latirostris*)," 1864, pp. 384-420.

33. "On a New Species of Grampus (*Orca meridionalis*), from Tasmania," 1864, pp. 420-426.

34. "Note on *Pseudorca meridionalis*," 1865, pp. 470-471.

35. "On *Physalus sibbaldii*, Gray," 1865, pp. 472-474.

36. "Observations upon a Fin-Whale (*Physalus antiquorum*, Gray) recently stranded in Pevensey Bay," 1865, pp. 699-705.

37. "On the Gular Pouch of the Great Bustard (*Otis tarda*, Linn.)," 1865, pp. 747-748.

38. "Note on the Visceral Anatomy of *Hyomoschus aquaticus*," 1867, pp. 954-960.

39. "On the Probable Identity of the Fin-Whales described as *Balænoptera carolinæ*, Malm., and *Physalus sibbaldii*, Gray," 1868, pp. 187-189.

40. "On the Development and Succession of the Teeth in the Armadillos," 1868, pp. 378-380.

41. "On the Value of the Characters of the Base of the Cranium in the Classification of the Order Carnivora, and on the Systematic Position of *Bassaris* and Other Disputed Forms," 1869, pp. 4-37.

42. "Note on a Substance Ejected from the Stomach of a Horn-bill," 1869, p. 150.

43. "On the Anatomy of the *Proteles cristatus*, Sparmann," 1869, pp. 474-496.

44. "Additional Note on a Specimen of the Common Fin-Whale (*Physalus antiquorum*, Gray, *Balænoptera musculus*, Auct.) Stranded in Langston Harbour, November 1869," 1870, pp. 330 and 331.

45. "On the Anatomy of *Ælurus fulgens*, Fr. Cuv.," 1870, pp. 752-769.

46. "On the Skeleton of the Australian Cassowary," 1871, pp. 32-35.

47. "On the Occurrence of the Ringed or Marbled Seal (*Phoca hispida*) on the Coast of Norfolk, with Remarks on the Synonymy of the Species," 1861, pp. 506-512.

48. "Remarks on a Rare Australian Whale of the Genus *Ziphius*," 1871, p. 631.

49. "Note on the Anatomy of the Two-Spotted Paradoxure (*Nandinia binotata*)," 1872, pp. 683 and 684.

50. "On the Structure and Affinities of the Musk-deer, (*Moschus moschiferus*, Linn.)," 1875, pp. 159-190.

51. "Description of the Skull of a Species of *Xiphodon*, Cuvier," 1876, pp. 3-7.

52. "On some Cranial and Dental Characters of the Existing Species of Rhinoceros," 1876, pp. 443-457.

53. "Remarks upon *Ziphius novæ-zealandiæ* and *Mesoplodon floweri*," 1876, pp. 477 and 478.

54. "On the Skull of a Rhinoceros (*R. lasiotis*, Scl.) from India," 1878, pp. 634-636.

55. "On the Common Dolphin (*Delphinus delphis*, Linn.)" 1879, pp. 382-384.

56. "Remarks upon a Drawing of *Delphinus tursio*," 1879, p. 386.

57. "Remarks upon the Skull of a Female Otaria (*Otaria gillespii*)," 1879, p. 551.

58. "Remarks upon the Skull of a Beluga, or White Whale (*Delphinapterus leucas*)," 1879, pp. 667-669.

59. "On the Cæcum of the Red Wolf (*Canis jubatus*, Desm.)," 1879, pp. 766 and 767.

60. "On the Bush-Dog (*Icticyon venaticus*, Lund)," 1880, pp. 70-76.

61. "On the Elephant-Seal (*Macrorhinus leoninus*, Linn.)," 1881, pp. 145-162.

62. "Notes on the Habits of the Manatee," 1881, pp. 453-456.

63. "On the Mutual Affinities of the Animals composing the Order Edentata," 1882, pp. 358-367.

64. "On the Cranium of a New Species of *Hyperöodon*, from the Australian Seas," 1882, pp. 392-396.

65. "On the Skull of a Young Chimpanzee," 1882, pp. 634-636.

66. "On the Whales of the Genus *Hyperöodon*," 1882, pp. 722-734.

67. "On the Arrangement of the Orders and Families of existing Mammalia," 1883, pp. 178-186.

68. "On the Characters and Divisions of the Family *Delphinidæ*," 1883, pp. 466-513.

69. "On a Specimen of Rudolphi's Rorqual (*Balænoptera borealis*, Lesson) lately taken on the Essex Coast," 1883, pp. 513-517.

70. "Remarks on the Burmese Elephant lately deposited in the Society's Gardens," 1884, p. 44.

71. "Remarks upon Four Skulls of the Common Bottle-nose Whale (*Hyperöodon rostratus*), showing the Development, with Age, of the Maxillary Crests," 1884, p. 206.

72. "Exhibition of a Mass of pure Spermaceti, obtained from the 'head-matter' of *Hyperöodon*," 1884, p. 206.

73. "Note on the Dentition of a young Capybara (*Hydrochærus capybara*)," 1884, pp. 252 and 253.

74. "Note on the Names of Two Genera of *Delphinidæ*," 1884, p. 417.

75. "Remarks upon a Specimen of Rudolphi's Rorqual

(*Balænoptera borealis*) taken in the Thames, 1887," p. 564.

76. "On the Pygmy Hippopotamus of Liberia (*Hippopotamus liberiensis*, Morton), and its Claims to Distinct Generic Rank," 1887, pp. 612-614.

77. "Remarks upon a Specimen of a Japanese Cock, with Elongated Upper Tail-coverts," 1888, p. 248.

78. "Remarks upon the Skin of the Face of a Male African Rhinoceros with a Third Horn," 1889, p. 448.

79. "Remarks upon a Photograph of the Nest of a Hornbill (*Tocus melanoleucus*), in which the Female was shown 'walled in,'" 1890, p. 401.

80. "Remarks on the Rules of Zoological Nomenclature," 1896, pp. 319-320.

e. In the "Natural History Review."

81. "On the Brain of the Siamang (*Hylobates syndactylus*, Raffles)," 1863, pp. 279-287.

82. "Note on the Number of Cervical Vertebræ in the Sirenia," 1864, pp. 259-264.

f. In the "Journal of Anatomy and Physiology."

83. "On the Homologies and Notation of the Teeth of the Mammalia," vol. iii. pp. 262-278 (1869); Abstract in *Rep. Brit. Assoc.*, vol. xxxviii. (Trans. of Sections), pp. 262-288 (1868).

84. "On the Composition of the Carpus of the Dog," series 2, vol. vi. pp. 62-64 (1870).

85. "On the Correspondence between the Parts Composing the Shoulder and the Pelvic Girdle of the Mammalia," vol. vi. pp. 239-249 (1870).

86. "Note on the Carpus of the Sloths," vol. vii. pp. 255 and 256 (1873).

g. In the "Quarterly Journal" of the Geological Society of London.

87. "On the Affinities and Probable Habits of the Extinct Australian Marsupial, *Thylacoleo carnifex*, Owen," vol. xxiv. pp. 307-319 (1868).

88. "Description of the Skull of a Species of *Halitherium* (*H. canhami*) from the Red Crag of Suffolk," vol. xxx. pp. 1-7 (1874).

89. "Note on the Occurrence of Remains of *Hyænarctos* in the Red Crag of Suffolk," vol. xxxiii. pp. 534-536 (1877).

h. In the "Proceedings" of the Royal Institution.

90. "On Palæontological Evidence of Gradual Modification of Animal Forms," vol. vii. pp. 94-104 (1873).

91. "The Extinct Animals of North America," vol. viii. pp. 103-105 (1876), and *Popular Science Review*, vol. xv. pp. 267-298 (1876).

92. "On Whales, Past and Present, and their Probable Origin," vol. x. pp. 360-376 (1883).

i. In the "Report" of the British Association for the Advancement of Science.

93. "On the Connexion of the Hyoid Arch with the Cranium," vol. xl. (Trans. of Sections), pp. 136 and 137 (1870).

94. "A Century's Progress in Zoological Knowledge," vol. xlviii., pp. 549-558 (1878), and *Nature*, vol. xviii. pp. 419-423 (1878).

j. In the Annals and Magazine of Natural History.

95. "On a Sub-Fossil Whale (*Eschrichtius robustus*) Discovered in Cornwall," ser. 4, vol. ix. pp. 440-442 (1872).

96. "Extinct Lemurina," ser. 4, vol. xvii. pp. 323-328 (1876).

k. In the "Journal" of the Royal Colonial Institute.

97. "Whales and Whale Fisheries": a Lecture delivered at the Royal Colonial Institute on 8th January 1885 (1885).

l. In Nature.

98. "On the Arrangement and Nomenclature of the Lobes of the Liver in Mammalia," vol. vi. pp. 346-365

(1872); and also *Rep. Brit. Assoc.*, vol. xlii. (Trans. of Sections), pp. 150 and 151 (1872).

99. "On the Ziphioid Whales," vol. v. pp. 103-106 (1872).

100. "Museum Specimens for Teaching Purposes," vol. xv. pp. 144-146, 184-186, and 204-206 (1876).

m. In the "Transactions" of the Geological Society of Cornwall.

101. "On the Bones of a Whale found at Petuan," 1872, 8 pp.

n. In the "Bulletin" of the Brussels Academy.

102. "Sur le basin et le fémur d'une Balénoptère," vol. xxi. pp. 131 and 132 (1866).

o. In the "Medical Times" and "Gazette."

103. "Comparative Anatomy," a Lecture, 1870.

104. "Lectures on the Comparative Anatomy of the Organs of Digestion of the Mammalia," delivered at the Royal College of Surgeons of England, in February and March 1872.

p. In the "Transactions" of the Odontological Society of London.

105. "On the First or Milk Dentition of the Mammalia," vol. iii. pp. 211-232 (1871).

106. "Note on the Specimens of Abnormal Dentition in the Museum of the Royal College of Surgeons," vol. xii. pp. 32-47 (1880).

q. In the "British Medical Journal."

107. "Dentition of the Mammalia," 1871.

108. "History of Extinct Mammals, and their Relation to Existing Forms," 1874.

109. "The Anatomy of the Cetacea and Edentata," 1881 and 1882.

r. In the " Encyclopædia Britannica," 9th Ed.

110. "The Horse," vol. xii. pp. 172-181 (1881).
111. "Mammalia" (*Insectivora, Chiroptera* and *Rodentia*, by G. E. Dobson), vol. xv. pp. 347-446 (1883).
112. "Whale," vol. xxiv. pp. 523-529 (1888).
And other articles.

s. In the " Report" of the Council of the Zoological Society.

113. "On the Progress of Zoology" : Address to the General Meeting held at the Society's Gardens, 16th June 1887. Appendix, 1887, pp. 37-67.

t. In the "Transactions" of the Middlesex Natural History Society.

114. "Horns and Antlers," 1887, pp. 1-10.

C. Anthropological Papers.

a. In the " Journal" of the Anthropological Institute.

115. "Illustrations of the Modes of Preserving the Dead in Darnley Island and in South Australia," vol. viii. pp. 389-394 (1879).
116. "On the Osteology and Affinities of the Natives of the Andaman Islands," vol. ix. pp. 108-135 (1879).
117. "On the Cranial Characters of the Natives of the Fiji Islands," vol. x. pp. 153-173 (1880).
118. "On a Collection of Monumental Heads and Artificially deformed Crania from the Island of Mallicollo, in the New Hebrides," vol. xi. pp. 75-81 (1881).
119. "On the Aims and Prospects of the Study of Anthropology," vol. xiii. pp. 488-501 (1884).
120. "Additional Observations on the Osteology of the Natives of the Andaman Islands," vol. xiv. pp. 115-120 (1884).

121. "On the size of the Teeth as a Character of Race," vol. xiv. pp. 183-186 (1884).

122. "On the Classification of the Varieties of the Human Species," vol. xiv. pp. 378-395 (1885).

122A. "On a Nicobarese Skull," vol. xvi. pp. 147-149 (1886).

123. "Description of two Skeletons of Akkas, a Pygmy Race from Central Africa," vol. xviii. pp. 3-19 (1888).

124. "On two Skulls from a Cave in Jamaica," vol. xx. pp. 110-112 (1890).

b. In the " Report " of the British Association.

125. "Methods and Results of Measurements of the Capacity of Human Crania," 1878, pp. 581, 582; and *Nature*, vol. xviii. pp. 480, 481 (1878).

126. "The Study and Progress of Anthropology" (Address to Anthrop. Dept. of Zoological Section), 1881, pp. 682-689; and *Nature*, vol. xxiv. pp. 436-439 (1881).

c. In " Nature."

127. "The Comparative Anatomy of Man" (Abstract of Lectures), vol. xx. pp. 222-225, 244-246 (1879), and 267-269; vol. xxii. pp. 59-61, 78-80, 97-100 (1880).

d. In the " British Medical Journal."

128. "The Anatomical Characters of the Races of Man," 1879 and 1880.

e. In the " Journal of Anatomy and Physiology."

129. "On the Scapular Index as a Race-Character in Man," vol. xiv., pp. 13-17 (1880), written in co-operation with Dr. J. G. Garson.

f. In the Manchester Science Lectures for the People.

130. "The Aborigines of Tasmania, an Extinct Race." A Lecture delivered in Hulme Town Hall, Manchester, 30th November 1878, ser. x. pp. 41-53.

g. In " Report" of Glasgow Science Lectures Association.

131. "The Races of Man," 53 pp. Glasgow (1878).

h. In the " Proceedings " of the Royal Institution.

132. "The Native Races of the Pacific Ocean," vol. viii. pp. 602-652 (1878).

133. "The Pygmy Races of Men," vol. xii. pp. 266-283 (1888).

D. On Museums and Museum Arrangements.

134. "The Museum of the Royal College of Surgeons of England." Presidential Address to the Anatomical Section of the International Medical Congress, held in London, 4th August 1881. [Reprinted in *Essays on Museums*, as are the other papers and addresses quoted under this heading.]

135. "Museum Organisation." Presidential Address to the British Association for the Advancement of Science, at the Newcastle-on-Tyne Meeting, 11th September 1889. *Rep. Brit. Assoc.*, 1889.

136. "School Museums : Suggestions for the Formation and Arrangement of Natural History in connection with a Public School." *Nature*, 26th December 1889.

137. "The Booth Museum." Address at the Opening of the Booth Museum, Brighton, 3rd November 1890. *Zoologist*, December 1890.

138. "Local Museums." From a letter in support of the establishment of a County Museum for Buckinghamshire (24th November 1891), and an Address at the Opening of the Perth Museum (29th November 1895).

139. "Modern Museums." Presidential Address to the Museums' Association, at the Meeting held in London, 3rd July 1893. *Museums' Association Journal*, 1893.

140. "Natural History as a Vocation (Boys' Museums)." *Chambers's Edinburgh Journal*, April 1897.

E. Biographical Sketches by Sir William Flower

Mostly Republished in " Essays on Museums."

141. "Biographical Notice of Professor Rolleston." *Proc. Roy. Soc.*, 1882.

142. Obituary Notice of George Busk. *Journ. Anthrop. Inst.*, vol. xvi., p. 403 (1886).

143. "Biographical Notice of Sir Richard Owen." *Proc. Roy. Soc.*, 1894.

144. "Reminiscences of Professor Huxley." *The North American Review*, September 1895.

145. "Eulogium on Charles Darwin." Centenary Meeting of the Linnean Society, 24th May 1888.

CPSIA information can be obtained
at www.ICGtesting.com
Printed in the USA
BVHW070915051218
534842BV00021B/391/P

9 781332 330430